"To the weak I became as weak, that I might gain the weak: I am made all things to all men, that I might by all means save some."
1 Corinthians 9:22

"As one whom his mother comforts, so I will comfort you, and you shall be comforted in Jerusalem." Isaiah, final chapter
"Happy Ending"

THE Marriage

KNOWLEDGE OF GOD TO TRUST IN GOD

LAURA CHRISTIAN

Copyright © 2025 Laura Christian.

All rights reserved. I love sharing my music, poetry, and the lessons God has taught me. All music featured at the end, along with my writings and reflections, are original works and are shared with love and purpose.

ISBN: 978-1-63950-349-0 (sc)
ISBN: 978-1-63950-363-6 (hc)
ISBN: 978-1-63950-348-3 (e)

Because of the dynamic nature of the Internet, any web addresses or links contained in this book may have changed since publication and may no longer be valid. The views expressed in this work are solely those of the author and do not necessarily reflect the views of the publisher, and the publisher hereby disclaims any responsibility for them.

Gateway Towards Success

8063 MADISON AVE #1252
Indianapolis, IN 46227
+13176596889
www.writersapex.com

Because He created the whole universe,

the whole world,

all things,

and me,

I dedicate this book to my Lord GOD.

To My Readers,

You can always fulfill the purpose of life no matter what is happening, because the purpose of life is to know God and to trust in Him. That can be done at all times, under any circumstance. We can be getting to know Him a little more in tiny ways, or we can be getting to know Him a lot more in big ways. It doesn't really matter, because He's the one that gets the attention, not us. He's the one that is important, not us, and God is a person, so the important thing is that we get to know His person more. So that has nothing to do with big and little, but just a sweet relationship with the Almighty God. Amen.

I finished this book about January 2008. I ended up making six copies and giving them to family and friends. This book in its original form was larger in size and larger in length, and full color, very artsy. I wanted to make it available to everybody, and in so doing, I turned it black and white and condensed it. As soon as possible I will make it available in my original form. In its original form it will be really expensive as a hardback or paperback, however as an ebook it will be very accessible.

I would like to apologize for any inaccuracies in my Bible quotes. Please feel free to look each one up on the internet under KJV, short for King James Version of the Bible.

Happy reading! ♡

Sincerely,

Laura Christian

Jesus said, "learn of me and I will give you rest unto your souls."

Now as I retype this to make it legible, I'd like to add that I'm remembering that I had an extremely firm revelation that I was dead to sin, but alive to God in Christ Jesus. I was trying to obey what the Apostle Paul said, "Consider yourselves dead indeed to sin, but alive to God in Christ Jesus." So I would walk around the Bible campus saying to myself, "I'm dead to sin, and alive to God in Christ Jesus." I said it constantly, until one day, and I remember where I was standing, it became a reality. I was truly dead to sin, and alive to God. I was free to think about God and get to know him without any interference.

Coffee Talk

I'd like to share with you as if over coffee. The truths that I so loving relate in this book I walked straight in for 21 years. I remember saying to myself, "This is so simple, I could never forget it." But such is not the case. God is the giver of all revelations, and as He gives, He can also take away, if He so chooses. I remember the Bible says, "I will cover her way with thorns and briers, and she shall not be able to find her paths."

About seven years ago, I actually forgot those truths God gave me, much as the blocks disassembled below, and try as I might, I could not regain or remember those truths. Scripture says, "Remember the old paths." I remembered how I use to have "a meek and quiet spirit which in the sight of the LORD is of great value." But I could not regain the simple bonding I had with God through these truths.

Last night about 1:00 in the morning (November 6, 2007) I began to have that bonding again, in fact, in the last couple of days I've had it a couple times. I've oddly remembered the "secret ingredient", as the Holy Scripture teaches, "the secret of the LORD is with them that fear Him."

I remembered the Holy Spirit was my constant teacher. I would indeed say to myself continually, "Know Jesus. Trust in Him." But the difference, I'm in the process of realizing, as I place the final page numbers in this book, page by page, with my "squigglys" on each side of each number, yesterday getting to 101, is that I waited on the Holy Spirit, quietly, to teach me and lead my thoughts.

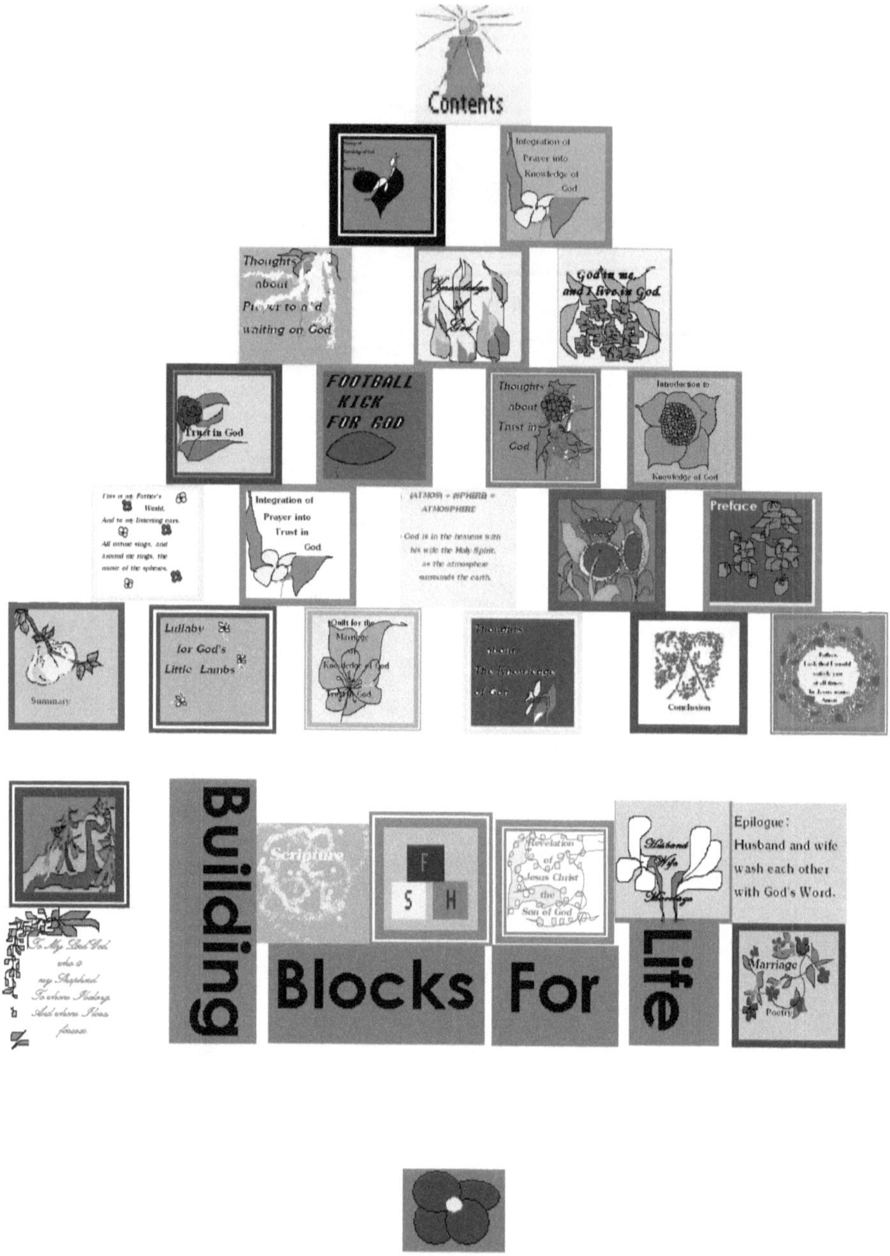

Contents
Integration of Prayer into Knowledge of God
Thoughts about Prayer to God waiting on God
God in me, and I live in God.
Trust in God
FOOTBALL KICK FOR GOD
Thoughts about Trust in God
Introduction to Knowledge of God
Integration of Prayer into Trust in God
(ATMOS) + (SPHERE) = ATMOSPHERE
God is in the heavens with his wife the Holy Spirit, as the atmosphere surrounds the earth.
Preface
Summary
Lullaby for God's Little Lambs
Thoughts about The Knowledge of God
Conclusion
Building Blocks For Life
Scripture
F S H
Revelation of Jesus Christ the Son of God
Epilogue:
Husband and wife wash each other with God's Word.
Marriage Poetry

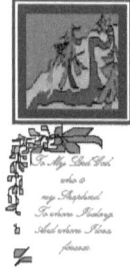

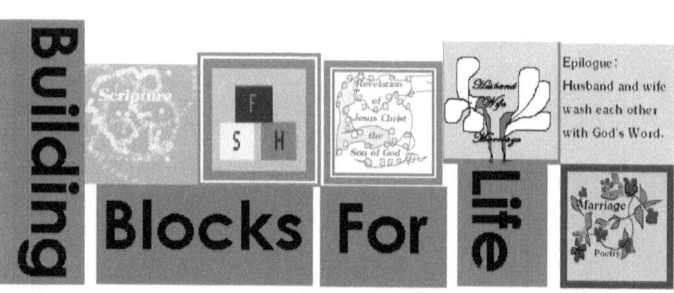

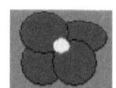

LAURA CHRISTIAN
THE MARRIAGE
KNOWLEDGE OF GOD
TO TRUST IN GOD

Preface 3
Marriage Partner, Knowledge of God 11
Introduction to Knowledge of God 13
Knowledge of God 23
Integration of Prayer into Knowledge of God 87
Conclusion 105
Summary 119
Marriage Partner, Trust in God 129
Introduction to Trust in God 131
Trust in God 135
Integration of Prayer into Trust in God 171
Conclusion 205
Summary 209
Marriage Celebration and Ceremony 217
Husband Wife Marriage 219
Epilogue: Husband and Wife Wash Each Other With God's Word 249
Thoughts About The Knowledge of God 267
Thoughts About Trust in God 273
Thoughts About Prayer To and Waiting on God 279
(THOUGHTS) + (POETRY) = THOUGHTOETRY 287

"In the beginning God created the heaven and the earth."
Bible, Old Testament, Genesis 1:1

"And I saw a new heaven and a new earth:
for the first heaven and the first earth were passed away;..."
Bible, New Testament, Revelation 21:1

The Marriage

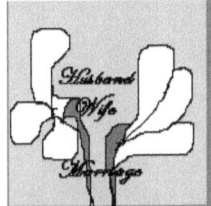

Knowledge of God

to

Trust in God

We know that whoever is born of God does not sin; but he that is born of God keeps himself, and that wicked one does not touch him. And we know that we are of God, and the whole world lies in wickedness. And we know that the Son of God is come, and has given us an understanding, that we may know him that is true, and we are in him that is true, even in his Son Jesus Christ. This is the true God, and eternal life. Little children, keep yourselves from idols. Amen."
Bible, New Testament, 1 John 5:18-21

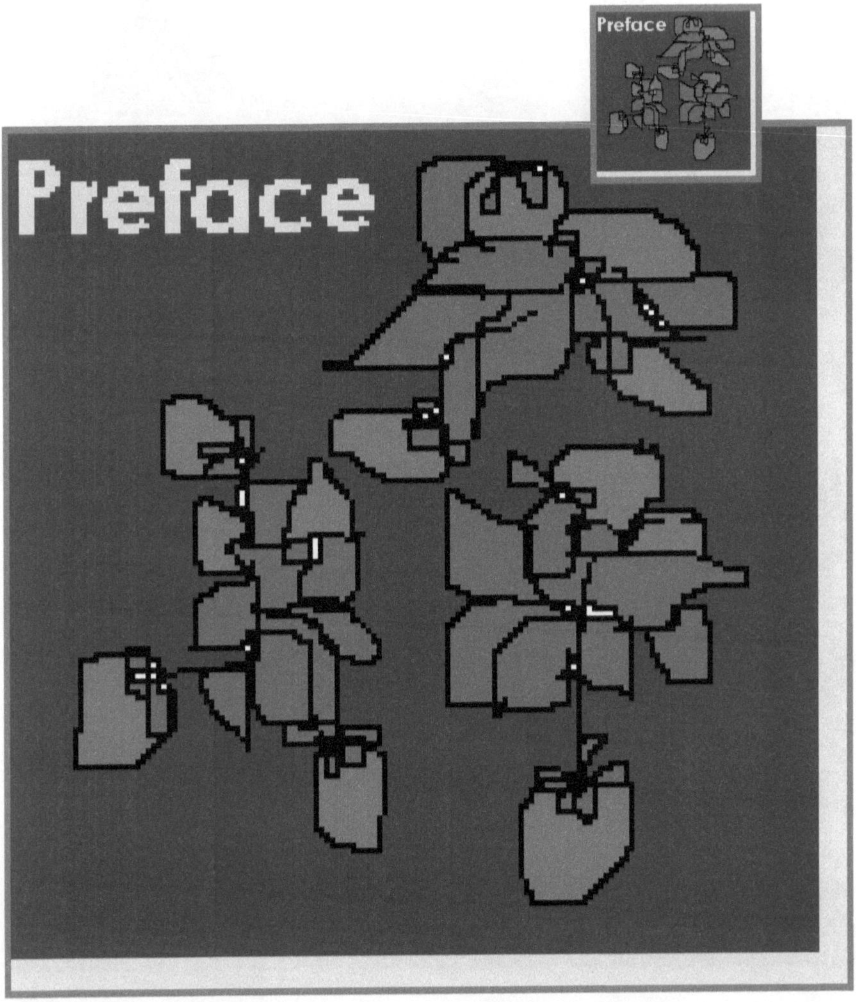

Preface

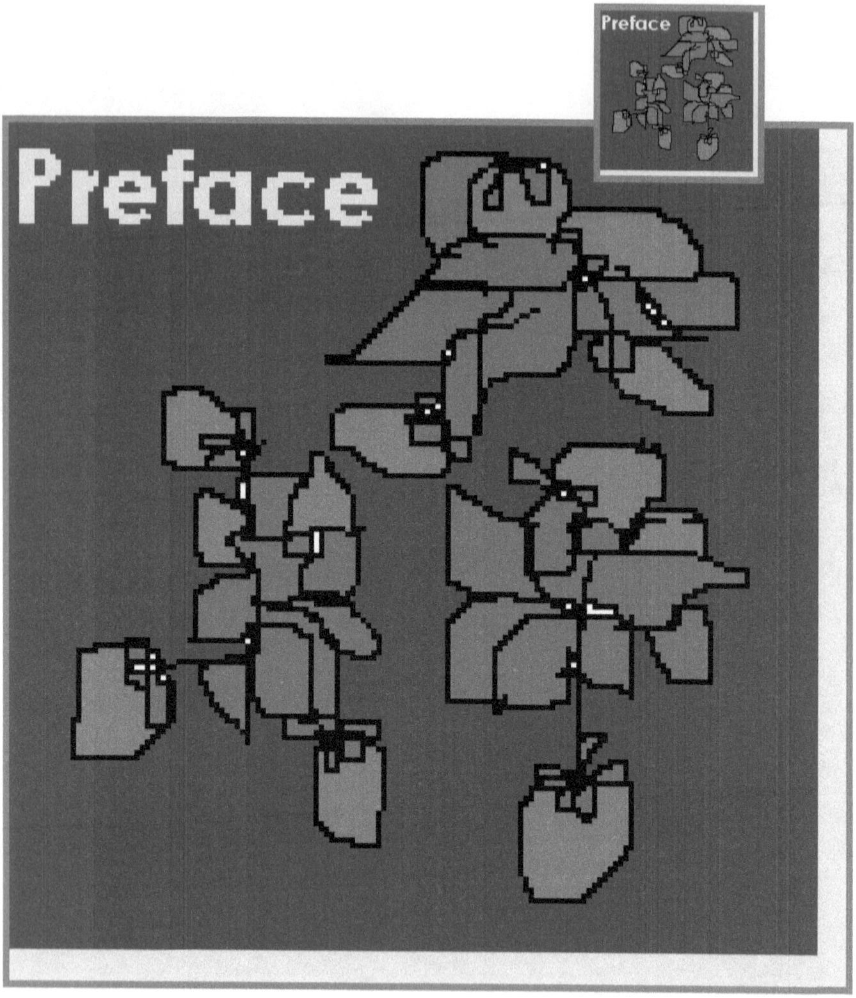

Preface

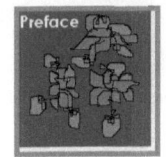

Preface

The root question buried in my heart and revealed in this book is, "How do I please God?"

I have discovered three ways to please God that I would like to discuss and ponder: **Knowledge of God, Trust in God,** and **Prayer to God**. Bible Scripture informs us with certainty that these <u>are</u> ways to please God. In this book the first two ways to please God, **Knowledge of God** and **Trust in God** are presented. At the end of each, ponderings about prayer are infused, a third way to please God. The two elements, **Knowledge of God** and **Trust in God**, although completely different avenues of thought, must be "married" to be fruitful. That is why I chose to call the title of this book, <u>The Marriage of Knowledge of God to Trust in God</u>. In the "Marriage", page 261, I share how this married couple are dependent one on another, as the heavens and the earth are dependent, and how to form a **POINT OF CONTACT** with God.

Preface

It is my desire to give an objective outlook of the subjects being presented, expressing and dealing with facts and conditions as perceived, without distortion by personal feelings, prejudice, or interpretation (Webster's definition of objective). **In this book are frequent references to the Bible. I use it in confidence as an indisputably reliable source of information.**

The subject matter I am presenting contains ideas that have been the center and core of my heart and belief system, and the foundation and purpose of my life since Winter Quarter at Bible College in 1976. That is when these truths became real and vital to me. I consider it a pivotal time in my life when God graciously granted these insights to me. As this door opened, I rushed through it with great rejoicing and ecstasy into a place where I could finally be free with God, having His peace, presence, and assurance with me at all times. My life became a very close, intimate, and content walk with God. Ever since, I am able to feel free in His presence. I have confidence at all times that I truly belong to God.

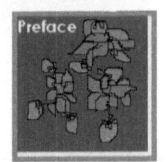

Preface

I know I am always pleasing to God when He sees childlike trust in me, and when I'm in simple trust, I know He considers me as perfect in His eyes. God released me into this life of trust after about six years of crying every night, literally or in my heart, knowing faith is required to get to Heaven and I didn't have it. Perhaps I struggled with faith because I grew up in a home filled with Science, my Dad being a devout Physicist. He would sign his poetry with the name, Phys. When God graciously granted me this life of trust, I heard Him say in my mind, "You have found the answer. Look no further. It is the final answer." I don't take the spiritual truths that I have found lightly, because they are my very life and breath, my comfort in sorrow, and my great joy in simple everyday existence and experiences. I now have inspiration to continually seek to attain to a greater and deeper quality of life, and develop and use any talents God has given to me, with great delight. I am now free in human relationships to appreciate others, develop relationships, enjoy my children, my extended family, the church family, and others in our community. These truths I delved into also have set me free from grievous mistakes, and the burden

of past failures and shortcomings. They have set me free to such an extent, that I don't carry these burdens anymore. Now I am able to completely release them to my loving Heavenly Father, not in an abstract way but in reality, on a moment to moment basis. They are real and effective. Their foundations and roots are in the Bible, the Word of the living God. These truths on which I now stabilize my life are not "mini-excerpts" from the Bible but are obtained from numerous readings, studies and meditations of whole books of the Bible in their entirety. I have come to the point of <u>knowing</u> what is being said in particular books of the Bible, and have full assurance and confidence that I comprehend exactly what was on the author's heart and mind and the complete conception of what he was trying to relate. When I explore truths in the Bible, I am not trying to prove anything, establish a theory, or gain knowledge just to have more knowledge. When I am in deep study, I read out of a personal passion to please God my lovely Savior, and friend.

God bless you.
I hope that this writing can somehow be a blessing to you.

Personal Notes, Thoughts

*"there is no truth, nor mercy,
nor knowledge of God in the land… My people are
destroyed for lack of knowledge: because
you have rejected knowledge,
I will also reject you,…"*
Hosea 4:1,6

Knowledge of God

*"And this is eternal life,
that they might know thee the only true God,
and Jesus Christ, whom thou hast sent."*
Before his 'Passion' and death
Jesus prayed this.
John 17:3

Introduction to Knowledge of God

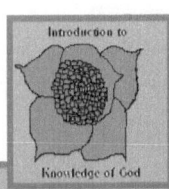

Introduction to Knowledge of God, Ponderings

All of life comes from God. God is life.

Knowledge of God is the fountain; foundation for all life.

To live eternally we must find God as our life, because we are not prepared to live as eternal beings with a perfect God. We are naturally sinful and separated from God, sinful to the core, from the womb. King David said, "Behold, I was shaped in iniquity; and in sin did my mother conceive me." (Psalm 51: 5). The Holy Spirit wrote through the prophet Jeremiah, " The heart <u>is</u> deceitful above all <u>things</u>, and desperately wicked: who can know it ?" He also wrote, "Blessed is the man that trusts in the LORD, and whose hope the LORD is." (Jeremiah 17: 9, 7). God says in the book of Isaiah, "I knew that you <u>are</u> obstinate, and your neck is an iron sinew, and your brow brass... your ear was not opened: for I knew you would deal very treacherously, and that you were called a transgressor from the womb. " (48:8).

Paul the Apostle, who wrote about 70% of the New Testament, and to whom God gave "daily, the care of all the churches." (II Corinthians 11:28), said about himself: "Concerning zeal, persecuting the church; touching the righteousness which is in the law, blameless." (Philippians 3: 4,6). But he also wrote: **"Christ Jesus came into the world to save sinners ; of whom I am chief."** (1 Timothy 1:15). So we need to find our way back to our loving and righteous God, to have life again and live forever. Jesus provided the way back to God, because He paid for the sins of all mankind. **"For he hath made him <u>to be</u> sin for us, who knew no sin; that we might be made the righteousness of God in him."** (2 Corinthians 5:21). Each of us are participants if we choose Him as our life, our spirit becoming one with His Spirit. We can ask Jesus into our hearts to be our own personal Savior. We need to invite Him in, because God is a gentleman. It's just like inviting someone into our home. One can do this by just saying a simple prayer. Our hearts are like our home into which we can invite the LORD, our Savior as our eternal guest.

We can pray:

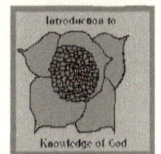

"Dear Heavenly Father,

Please come into my heart Jesus,
to be my own personal Savior.

You are welcome here.
Thank you for dying on the cross for my sins,

and that your blood makes
all mankind perfect forever, including me.

Thank you that you took away all the sins of
all mankind, including mine.

Thank you that when you came alive,
all mankind came alive with you, including me,

free from all darkness, hate, the sinful nature,
and all evil tendencies.

Thank you that you conquered sin,

the sin nature, sickness, death, Hell, and the Devil.

Thank you that you conquered

all these things for all of us.

Thank you that you have come into my heart, just as I asked you to. You said in Luke 11:11-13:

"If a son asks bread of any of you that is a father,
will you give him a rock?
Or if <u>he asks</u> for fish, will you give him a snake?
Or if he asks for an egg,
will you offer him a scorpion?
If you then being evil,
know how to give good gifts to your children:
how much more shall <u>your</u> Heavenly Father
give the Holy Spirit
to them that ask him."

Thank you Father,

that now I belong to you,

You now live in my heart by your Holy Spirit.

I am now your child and a member of your very own family.

Let me read your word faithfully because,

the Bible says in II Peter 2:2, "As newborn babies,

desire the sincere milk of the Word,

that you may grow from it," and Jesus you said,

"Man shall not live by bread alone but by every word that comes out of the mouth of God."

Please give me a church to attend,

that faithfully follows your Word,

and please give me two or three close friends,

of my own gender, that also have invited you into their hearts,

and want to grow in you, because you said:

> *"When two or three of you*
> *are gathered together,*
> *there I am in your midst."*

Thank you Heavenly Father.

Thank you Jesus.

Thank you Holy Spirit.

I am always brand new in you. I love you.

> *In Jesus' name I pray, Amen."*

That was a lengthy prayer. A short one is fine.

The Scripture (the Bible) says, "It shall come to pass, <u>that</u> whoever shall call on the name of the Lord shall be saved." (Acts 2: 21). So a person may just call on His name, "Jesus," and be saved, or say simply, "Please come in my heart Jesus," and He will gladly come in. Jesus also said in Revelation 3:20,

"See, I stand at the door, and knock:
If any man hears my voice, and opens the door,
I will come into him,
and will eat with him, and he with me."

Through the prophet Isaiah, God actually makes a statement of astonishing boldness concerning the simplicity of receiving Him. He says the whole world can be saved just by looking at Him!!! This amazing Scripture is found in Isaiah 45: 21-24. "…who has declared this from ancient time? Who has told it from that time? Have not I the LORD? And there is no God else beside me; a just God and a Savior; there is none beside me. Look to me, and be saved, all the ends of the earth; for I am God, and there is none else. I have sworn by myself, the word is gone out of my mouth in righteousness, and shall not return, that to me every knee shall bow, every tongue shall swear. Surely, shall one say, in the LORD have I righteousness and strength; even to him shall men come; and all that are incensed against him shall be ashamed."

After asking Jesus into our hearts, we are reconciled to God. To live in God, we need to learn about Him, delight to get to know Him, and learn to trust Him forever, as a little child in his Father's arms. We also need to learn to spend time waiting quietly on Him in prayer. Jesus said,

*Fear not little flock;
for it is your Father's good pleasure
to give you the kingdom."*

*This is eternal life,
that they may know you
the only true God,
and Jesus Christ,
whom you have sent."*

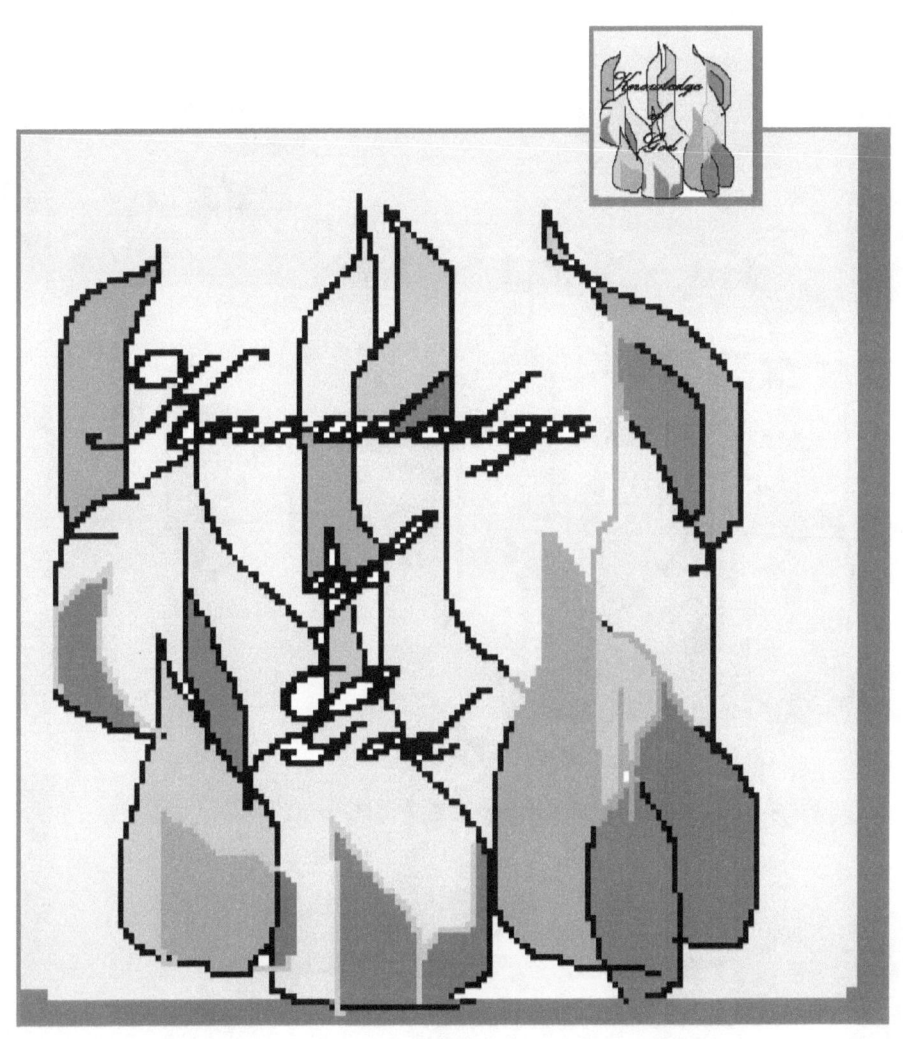

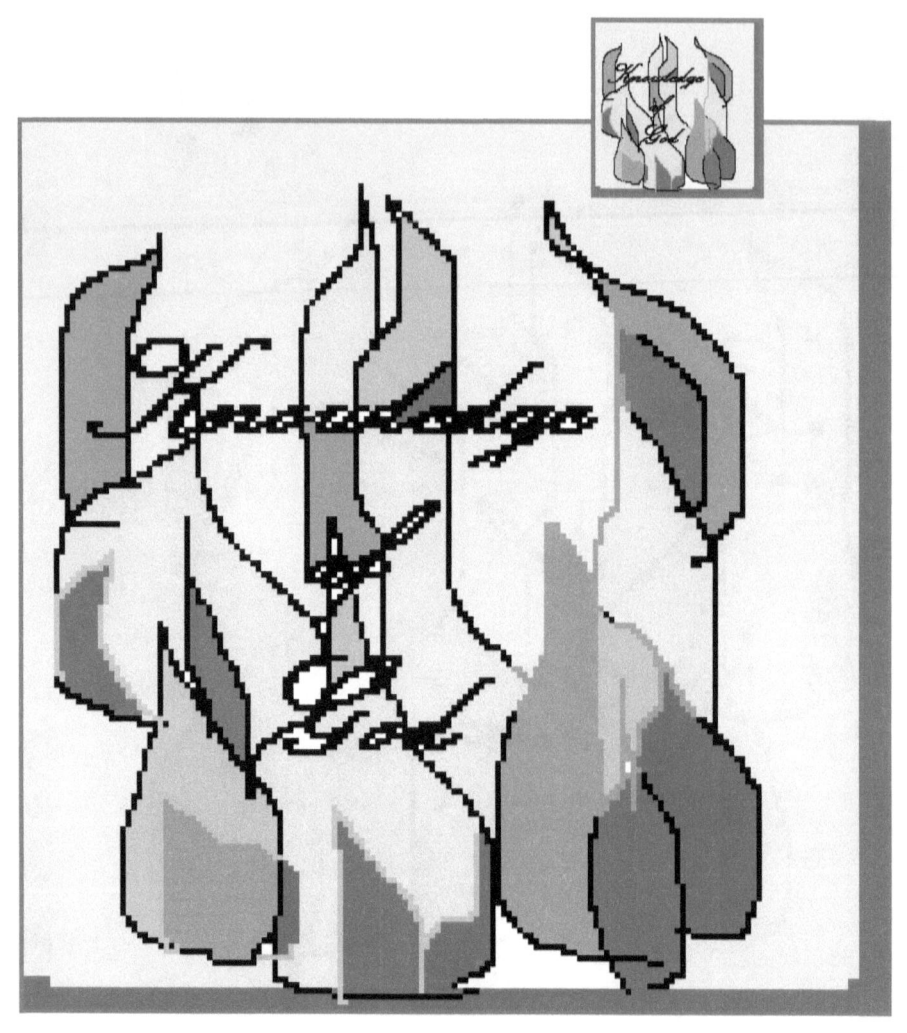

Knowledge of God, Ponderings

The **Knowledge of God** is an essential ingredient to mix with **Trust in God**, otherwise we will be having faith and trust in a God of our own making that does not even exist. We will be believing in an imaginary god. There will be no stability and no security, because when our imagination ceases to exist, so will the imaginary god cease to exist that we created in our minds.

Since we are God's creations of free-will choice, with freedom given to us by a loving God, we can do anything we wish. However, if we choose rebellion against Him, we will be chastised by a loving Heavenly Father who will try to reclaim us from darkness, and who patiently waits for us to use our freedom to return to the light, to Him. At the Judgement we will each stand alone before our Creator to give an account of what we have done, or haven't done. If we know Him, the Holy Scripture teaches, our useless works will be burned up like hay, wood, and stubble and our eternal works will remain forever, like gold, silver, and precious stones that remain, although they go through the fire.

But because of the precious gift of free-will choice God has given to us, we can think anything we want to about Him. We can even think that He does not exist. We can form in our minds any thought we want to, and think Him to be like we wish He would be, and think Him to be like us. But if we do, we have no knowledge of, or trust in the real God, that **really** exists.

The only way to get to know God is <u>objectively</u>, not subjectively. Because subjectively, we are subject to our own whims, wants, desires, dislikes, ideas, comprehensions, outlooks, senses, and the limits of our own intellect and spiritual understanding.

Since we are natural creations, we <u>really</u> cannot attain to the true **Knowledge of God**. The true **Knowledge of God** is what **really** goes on in God's <u>own</u> heart, God's <u>own</u> mind, and God's <u>own</u> desires.

Man cannot reach God on his own strength or merit.

Man's thoughts cannot aspire to God's thoughts. In Scripture, Isaiah 55: 8,9 God says, "For your thoughts are not my thoughts, neither are your ways my ways, says the LORD. For as the heavens are higher than the earth, so are my ways higher than your ways, and my thoughts than your thoughts." The only way to attain to God's thoughts is to make use of the Holy Scripture He has put into the world, the Bible.

If one wants to know God, one must decide he would rather think God's thoughts instead of his own, which really is a spectacular decision, and a wonder that we can actually put God's thoughts into our own brains. But it really is true, and extremely simple.

A child can do it, by learning a little Scripture like, "**God is love.**" (1 John 4: 8).

Knowledge of God, gaining **Knowledge of God**, and increasing in **Knowledge of God**, goes on forever for there is no end to God or to His unexplainable wonders.

There is no end to His depth of character and beautiful emotions. He has the full range of human emotion like a huge rainbow, in the same way we experience emotions, because He was the one that made them, but He has no sin or darkness in His emotions. We were created in His image. Everything came out of His heart and mind. He couldn't make emotions if He didn't have them.

Getting to know God <u>is</u> eternal life. That is what Jesus said in His prayer to His Heavenly Father before He died for us, recorded by Jesus' close friend John. We find it in John 17:3,

"And this is life eternal, that they might know you the only true God, and Jesus Christ, whom you have sent."

So moments we spend getting to know Him, we are actually living in eternal life. Are we now presently doing so?

Putting Scripture in our minds is essential, because it is the true knowledge of the true God. In this way we can become acquainted with the **real** God that **really** exists, not one of our own making to cater to our own wishes, behaviors and emotions. Not a god of our imagination, but the **real** God of heaven and earth, and of the entire universe, that created everything with the words of His mouth. In the longest chapter of the Bible, Psalms 119, **King David** devoted all 176 verses to establishing the supremacy of the Word of God. In every single verse, the majesty of God's Word is declared. **Moses** and **Jesus** also spoke of the supremacy of God's Holy Word and the utter necessity of putting the words of God in our hearts and minds:

"GIVE ear, O you heavens, and I will speak;

and hear, O earth, the words of my mouth.

My doctrine shall drop as the rain, my speech

shall distil as the dew, as the small rain

on the tender herb, and as the showers on the grass:

Because I will publish the name of the LORD:

ascribe greatness to our God.

observe to do,

all the words of this law.

For it is not a vain thing for you;

because it is your life: and

through this thing you shall

prolong your days in the land,

where you go over Jordan to

possess it.

And the LORD spoke to Moses

that very same day, saying,

Get up into this mountain

Abarim, to mount Nebo,

which is in the land of Moab,

that is over against Jericho;

and see the land of Canaan,

which I give to the children of

Israel for a possession:

And die in the mount

where you go up,

and be gathered to your people ;

as Aaron your brother

died in mount Hor,

and was gathered

to his people :"

Deuteronomy 32:1- 4, 44-50

And Jesus said,

"It is written,
Man shall not live
by bread alone,

but by every word
that proceeds
out of the mouth of
God."

Matthew 4:4

We can also get to know the real God as He really is through His creation. The Scripture says that the creation speaks out God's Word continually, so we are without excuse for not worshiping God. Mankind has fallen, but God reaches out to us in our weak, sinful, and evil condition through Knowledge of God and Trust in God, that is, faith in Christ.

The following is written by Paul the Apostle who said: "But now I go to Jerusalem to minister to the saints." Romans 15:25, 1:20-32, 3:10-31

"For the invisible things of him from the creation of the world are clearly seen, being understood by the things that are made, <u>even</u> his eternal power and Godhead; so that they are without excuse: because that, when they knew God, they glorified <u>him</u> not as God neither were thankful; but became vain in their imaginations, and their foolish heart was darkened. Professing themselves to be wise, they became fools, and changed the glory of the incorruptible God into an image made like to corruptible man, and to birds, and four footed beasts, and creeping things. So God also gave them up to uncleanness, through the lusts of their own hearts, to dishonor their own bodies between themselves: who changed the truth of God into a lie, and worshiped and served the creature more than the Creator, who is blessed for ever. Amen. For this cause God gave them up to vile affections: for even women did change the natural use to that which is against nature. And likewise also the men, leaving the natural use of the women, burned in their lust one toward another; men with men working that which is unseemly, and receiving in themselves that recompense of their error which was meet. And even as they did not like to retain God in <u>their</u> knowledge, God gave them over to a reprobate mind, to do those things which are not

convenient; being filled with all unrighteousness, fornication, wickedness, covetousness, maliciousness; full of envy, murder, debate, deceit, malignity; whisperers, backbiters, haters of God, spiteful, proud, boasters, inventors of evil things, disobedient to parents, without understanding, covenant breakers, without natural affection, implacable, unmerciful: Who, knowing the judgement of God, that they which commit such things are worthy of death, not only do the same, but have pleasure in them that do them....As it is written, There is none righteous, no, not one: There is none that understands, there is none that seeks after God. They are all gone out of the way, they are together become unprofitable; there is none that does good, no, not one. Their throat is an open sepulcher; with their tongues they have used deceit; the poison of wasps is under their lips: whose mouth is full of cursing and bitterness: their feet are swift to shed blood: destruction and misery are in their ways: and the way of peace they have not known: there is no fear of God before their eyes. Now we know that whatever things that the law says, it says to them who are under the law: that every mouth may be stopped, and all the world may become guilty before God. Therefore by the works of the law there shall no flesh be justified in his sight: for by the law is the knowledge of sin. But now the righteousness of God without the law is manifested, being witnessed by the law and the prophets; even the righteousness of God which is by faith of Jesus Christ to all and upon all them that believe; for there is no difference. For all have sinned, and come short of the glory of God; being justified freely by his grace through the redemption that is in Christ Jesus: whom God has set forth to be a propitiation through faith in his blood, to declare his righteousness for the remission of sins that are past, through the forbearance of God; To declare, I say, at this time his righteousness: that he might be just, and the justifier of him which believes in Jesus. Where is boasting then ? It is excluded. By what law? Of works? No; but by the law of faith. Therefore we conclude that a man is justified by faith without the works of the law... Do we then make void the law through faith? God forbid: yes, we establish the law."

"The heavens declare the glory of God; and the firmament shows his handiwork. Day to day utters speech, and night to night shows knowledge. There is no speech or language, where their voice is not heard."

Psalm 19:1-3

Personal Notes, Thoughts

Since each of us are made in God's image, we can also get to know God by seeing Him and His wondrous works in ourselves and each other, minus any thoughts or behaviors that do not match God's character. God's glorious creation is at it's peak in us, as we look at each other, seeing God and His handiwork in one another.

And that is what life's really all about, recognizing and seeing God in all His creation around us, in each other and in His Holy Scriptures, and being deeply excited to get to know Him better, and more and more.

If we don't like His Holy Scriptures, like the parts about God's judgments, then we have decided not to get to know the real God, that really exists, as He really is. His Holy Scriptures reveal to us God's likes and dislikes, loves and hatreds.

Although God judges unrighteousness, cruelty, man's injustice to man, sin, etc., He has provided full provision for an escape from all His judgments. This provision is in His Son Jesus Christ, who took all of mankind's punishment on

Himself and all mankind's sin into His own being and body during His death on the cross. That is why Scripture says in the New Testament,

> *Jesus Christ . . .*
> *him that loved us,*
> *and washed us from our sins*
> *in his own blood."*

When Jesus hung on the cross for us, Scripture says he actually became sin, "For he has made him <u>to be</u> sin for us, who knew no sin" (2 Cor. 5:21), and took all the evil of mankind, and the sin nature, "the old man", to the grave. When he came alive, rising from the dead, Jesus brought all mankind up from the dead with him, perfectly brand new (about 2,000 years ago)! God reveals this through Paul the Apostle, writing while inspired by the Holy Spirit:

"What shall we say then? Shall we continue in sin, that grace may abound? God forbid. How shall we, that are dead to sin live any longer therein? Don't you know, that so many of us as were baptized into Jesus Christ were baptized into his death? Therefore we are buried with him by baptism into death; that like as Christ was raised up from the dead by the glory of the Father, even so we also should walk in newness of life. For if we have been planted together in the likeness of his death, we shall be also <u>in the likeness</u> of his resurrection: knowing this, that our old man is crucified with <u>him</u> that the body of sin might be destroyed, that from now on we should not serve sin. Now if we be dead with Christ, we believe that we shall also live with him; Knowing that Christ being raised from the dead dies no more; death has no more dominion over him. For in that he died, he died to sin once; but in that he lives, he lives to God. Likewise, consider also yourselves to be dead indeed to sin, but alive to God through Jesus Christ our Lord." . . . "And if Christ be in you, the body is dead because of sin; but the Spirit is life because of righteousness. But if the Spirit of him that raised up Jesus from the dead lives in you, he that raised up Christ from

the dead shall also quicken your mortal bodies by his Spirit that lives in you." (Romans 6:1-11 and 8:10,11). "For in Christ Jesus...a new creature. And as many as walk according to this rule, peace <u>be</u> on them, and mercy, and upon the Israel of God." (Galatians 6:15,16). So we see from Scripture that we are presently dead to sin, now alive to God in Christ Jesus, <u>were</u> risen from the dead <u>with</u> him, and so we <u>are</u> perpetually brand new. God has not kept back knowledge of Himself from us, it is we ourselves who <u>haven't chosen</u> to explore the revelations He has given to us about Himself. We <u>haven't chosen</u> to increase in the **Knowledge of God** and expound it to others. We should be thrilled to get to know our Creator, be thrilled that He would even want us to get to know Him, and that we would even be able to get to know Him. Because of God's righteousness and demand for perfection, purity, and holiness it is a wonder and...

amazing that we could even approach God without being burned up!

"For our God is a consuming fire."
Hebrew 12:29

Because of what Jesus did by dying for us and now living in our hearts by His Holy Spirit when we invited Him into our hearts to be our own personal Savior, we can approach God and come to Him without fear. In fact, we can nestle up to God, drawing ever nearer to Him.

But there is a danger that we would seek to draw near God on our own merit. God does not accept this.

He does accept childlike trust. That is the subject of the second part of this book, **Trust in God**, the marriage partner to **Knowledge of God**.

Apostle Paul also writes in Romans 9:30-33 and 10:1-4:

"What shall we say then? That the Gentiles, which followed not after righteousness, have attained to righteousness, even the righteousness which is of faith. But Israel, which followed after the law of righteousness, has not attained to the law of righteousness. Why? Because they sought it not by faith, but as it were by the works of the law.

For they stumbled at that stumblingstone;
As it is written, See, I lay in Zion
a stumblingstone and rock of offense:
and whoever believes on him
shall not be ashamed.

Brothers and sisters, my heart's desire and prayer to God for Israel is, that they may be saved. For I bear them record that they have a zeal of God, but not according to knowledge. For they being ignorant of God's righteousness, and going about to establish their own righteousness, have not submitted themselves to the righteousness of God.

For Christ is the end of the law for righteousness to every one that believes."

If we seek to **Trust in God**, but do not seek to gain **Knowledge of God**, then we will be putting our trust in an imaginary God of our own making that cannot help or save us.

Knowledge of God is like an addition or multiplication equation with no negative numbers. It is always increasing in the one who seeks **Knowledge of God** and it builds on the **Knowledge of God** to which he has already attained, and it gets bigger and greater, deeper and higher, wider and longer, continually and forever.

The amazing thing is that **God never gets boring**. Nothing about Him is boring, staid, or dull. You can see this by just looking at a buttercup or elephant, grasshopper or giraffe, hippo or whale, huge icebergs crashing down and breaking up into the open sea, or little children giggling with ice cream on their faces. His beauty is everywhere. If we had been blind all of our lives and

suddenly our eyes were opened, it would seem as if a <u>paradise</u> or ~ *a wonderland* ~ had opened up to us. There are wonders all around us, but they become meaningless if we don't see Jesus, our loving God, shining through each one.

Having Knowledge of God lifts us up over sorrows and defeat, even our own failures and defects. If the purpose of our life, and the purpose of life itself, is to know God, then when faced with sorrow, we are to look into His face, looking at the beauty of our loving God. As we gaze at His beauty all around us and in us, and appreciate His wonders in His own creation, then we <u>are</u> looking into His face. It is an expression of God's heart, and comes from His heart. We know through looking at God, that someday all sorrow will disappear forever, when He creates the new heavens and new earth, as He promised He would. We will all live forever there, enjoying His beauty and free from all care.

For, behold, I create new heavens and a new earth: and the former shall not be remembered, nor come into mind.
Isaiah 65:17

For as the new heavens and the new earth, which I will make, shall remain before me, saith the LORD, so shall your seed and your name remain.
Isaiah 66:22

Personal Notes, Thoughts

We also know that someday we will all be perfect and complete, able to enjoy life to its fullest, in its perfection, and relax in God's person and presence forever, where there is eternal ecstasy and security. 1 John 2:2 says,

> *"...we know that, when he shall appear, we shall be like him, for we shall see him as he is."*

We also know that God desires to fill us up, not with sorrow but with Himself, although we may be filled with sorrow at times when we see or experience the suffering of others, or experience suffering ourselves.

But nevertheless, God still desires us to be filled up with Himself and with His joy, so that in times of sorrow we can look at Him, and be <u>comforted</u>, and remain filled with His beauty and grace, even during times and periods of "gross darkness."

> *"the darkness shall cover the earth, and gross darkness the people; but the LORD shall arise upon you, and his glory shall be seen upon you."*
> *Isaiah 60:2*

We are pulled and drawn inside of God when we gaze upon His beauty, His face. His beauty can come through all of our sense gates: taste, smell, touch, sight, and hearing. Also, we can observe and experience His beauty, presence and love in us and through us, as we choose to do anything that matches His divine character, which is within us.

> *"To whom God would make known what is the riches of the glory of this mystery . . . which is Christ in you, the hope of glory."*
> *Colossians 1:27*

Indeed, His own divine nature does live within us.

When we do something in His likeness, for example, helping an elderly woman with her groceries across a busy street, we gain knowledge of God's characteristic of deep compassion and grow in **Knowledge of God**. We have experienced, even through our own bodies what God is like, by doing a kind action.

However, if we helped this same elderly woman across the street to gain "brownie points", build our own character and improve our own reputation we push away Knowledge of God from us, for we are thinking of our self instead of God.

Scripture confirms authoritatively that God doesn't accept anyone because of any good thing they have done, as Abraham found. **Abraham found something!!! What did Abraham find???** Apostle Paul writes: "What shall we say then that Abraham our father as pertaining to the flesh, has found? For if Abraham were justified by works, he has somewhat to glory; but not before God. For what says the scripture? Abraham believed God, and it

was counted to him for righteousness. Now to him that works is the reward not reckoned of grace, but of debt. But to him that works not, but believes on him that justifies the ungodly, his faith is counted for righteousness. Even as David also describes the blessedness of the man, to whom God imputes righteousness without works,

"'Blessed are they whose iniquities are forgiven, and whose sins are covered. Blessed is the man to whom the Lord will not impute sin.'"

Romans 4:1-7

God is pleased when we simply trust in His grace and what He has done for us, and magnify His goodness. Apostle Paul speaks again, "Knowing that a man is not justified by the works of the law, but by the faith of Jesus Christ, even we have believed in Jesus Christ, that we might be justified by the faith of Christ, and not by the works of the law: for by the works of the law shall no flesh be justified." (Galatians 2:16).

So **Knowledge of God** can't and doesn't include knowledge of ourselves. We read,

The loftiness of man shall be bowed down and the haughtiness of men shall be made low and the LORD alone shall be exalted in that day."

Isaiah 2:17

This also sets us free from being manipulated and controlled by others, because if we are preoccupied with getting to know God's person, no one else's person will infect our minds, senses and beings. It truly is an infection when this happens, because <u>their</u> person takes the place of God's person in our hearts.

We were created to worship God and adore Him, not a person other than God. If we are busy worshiping and adoring another person, then there is no longer any room in that secret place of our heart for God. The attention that belongs to God's person, then, we are giving to another person who is exalting himself against the **Knowledge of God**.

Then we have to choose. Would we rather get to know the person that is trying to get attention, exalt himself and magnify human flesh, or do we choose to spend our eternity getting to know God, giving our attention, focus, energy, attraction, and yearnings to Him, our Creator?

And God *truly* is a person. For He could not create a person, if He were not Himself a person.

And God is a loving person, and cares about us. And God is a beautiful person, righteous, holy and pure. And God desires to be our friend, and desires to be the fulfillment of our every desire, inner longings and loneliness.

How could a person think that God could not fill up their loneliness when God Himself is love? He is love, and is ever and always overflowing with tenderness and compassion.

If we choose *not* to get to know God, we have chosen *not* to get to know our best friend, our own dear Heavenly Father.

That is an unfortunate choice, and *may result in our not making Heaven our home.*

If we fill ourselves up with the knowledge of self and others, there is no more room for **Knowledge of God**, just like there was no room for baby Jesus in the Inn, when his mother was about to give birth.

✡ **Our hearts are like the Inn of Bethlehem.** ✡

✡ **Is there any room?** ✡

Each one of us can choose to fill our inward being with other people. But then there is no more room left for baby Jesus, who desires to be birthed in our hearts. Apostle Paul said,

*"My little children,
of whom I travail in birth again
until Christ be formed in you,"
Galatians 4:19*

Some people spend their entire lifetimes trying to get attention. This gets extremely difficult if we are under their influence, because they will earnestly, continually, and actively endeavor to fill up our lives and senses with themselves. These kind of people will do anything to get our attention on them.

This may include trying to create sorrow, or on the other hand, trying to create joy. But whatever they do, it is for themselves. It is for the purpose of getting our mind's eye on them and getting us filled up with them, <u>not God</u>, getting us filled up with their person, <u>not</u> God's person.

In these cases if one still wants to follow Christ and the **Knowledge of God**, it's best, as far as I can tell, to seek how to be preoccupied with getting to know God and trusting in Him. We can seek to be always and actively engaging our minds and **exercising** our senses, meditations, and free-will choice to **choose God**, to **choose God and His goodness**.

We can develop our ability to focus on God, and rest in His presence, growing in **Knowledge of God** and our ability to trust in Him. This is a learning process, and requires earnest fortitude and focus (that is, for we adults). As it says in Hebrews 4:11, "Let us labor therefore to enter into that rest."

Little children show natural expertise at absorbing God's wonders, and these are full of the **Knowledge of God**. They just focus on what is before them in fascination, and are not pulled away by people's opinions and efforts to gain attention.

Little children are preoccupied with looking at a bright color or shape, and are not developed enough in human thinking to consider the opinions and mindsets of others.

Little children are captivated and taken up by God's good creation all around them. Infants are <u>satisfied</u> as they absorb the wonders, beauties and goodness of God!

"I will mention the lovingkindnesses of the LORD, and the praises of the LORD, according to all that the LORD has bestowed on us, and the great goodness toward the house of Israel, which he has bestowed on them according to his mercies, and according to the multitude of his lovingkindnesses."

Isaiah 63:7

Personal Notes, Thoughts

We too should be so simple indeed, to be so excited to get to know our Creator God in brand new ways, and brand new experiences, all the time, all around us! Yes, we can, and should be captivated with the smallest, most insignificant parts of God's good creation because these tiny things are teaching us about a great, big, gigantic, all powerful, all knowing, everywhere God who created everything, and could "uncreate" everything for that matter; a God who is love and whose wonders are ever enfolding and unfolding. God embraces us through His wonders and is always blossoming, expanding and unwrapping new things!

Perhaps we too <u>can</u> begin to magnify God, our only true friend, and the only true person that is eternal. It is <u>only</u> as we see and acknowledge God's person in ourselves and others that we have true life.

God lives in those who have received Jesus Christ as their personal Savior. Apostle Paul stated that he no longer lived:

"I am crucified with Christ: nevertheless I live; yet not I, but Christ lives in me: and the life which I now live in the flesh I live by the faith of the Son of God, who loved me, and gave himself for me. I do not frustrate the grace of God: for if righteousness comes by the law, then Christ died in vain."

Gal. 2:20.21

There are so many joys in life of which we do not avail ourselves. Plato spoke truth when he said, "Remember how in that communion only, beholding beauty with the eye of the mind, he will be enabled to bring forth, not images of beauty, but realities (for he has hold not of an image but of a reality), and bringing forth and nourishing true virtue to become the friend of God and be immortal..." (Symposium). Figuratively, if one were a photographer, one could sit in one place forever, and take endless pictures of little things, like grass, clouds, branches of trees, leaves, bugs, people, and get different angles, shadings, and colors, and focus on different shapes. There is truly beauty all around us of which we do not avail ourselves or, "behold". We do not focus in on it because we have no reason or incentive to do so. Is this because our hearts yearn for love, compassion, companionship and a person who will care for us and we for them? But that person is God. And that person, God, is talking to us, and that person God, is showing His love for us through each and every little thing He made for us.

And that person...

God, is personal and He does love each one of us in a personal way. He doesn't love anyone any more than anyone else. He loves each of us the same amount,

WITHOUT MEASURE.

He made everything for one of us, and that is the same amount He loves every one of us. He has poured out all His love into one, and that is the height, depth, length and breadth to which He loves every one of us individually, without exception.

Not one of us is loved by God more than another. If He singles out one of us, giving one person special things, and pours Himself out in unique blessings to a single individual, it is for the purpose of teaching all of us the extent to which He loves each one of us. **So there is, and should be, no jealousy in the body of Christ in anyone!!!**

We should just be pleased to know, that is how much He loves each of us. It is God's great passion to demonstrate His deep love for us. This is the only way we can understand the amount that He loves every one of us: for Him to give something special to one person.

When He does this we can look at others and think, <u>without being mistaken</u>, "That is how much God loves me! My own dear God is showing me how much He loves me!"

If God were to pour Himself out in the same way to all, it would not be as strong, potent, or concentrated a message as God giving all His attention to one. <u>Who could imagine that God, the great Creator would give all His attention to one?</u> But this is not an insult to any one of us. It is a compliment. It is to show the <u>degree and the extent</u> to which He loves every one of us. It is the only way for us to grasp and understand the depth, passion, fervency, degree, dedication, commitment and faithfulness that He has towards each of us, individually.

How else could we understand? If God is willing to pour Himself out and funnel all His love <u>into one person forever</u>, then He would be willing to do that for <u>any of us</u>. He is showing the degree to which He actually loves each one of us, by actually carrying it out and demonstrating it in reality, forever.

Since mankind is one, then we are all partakers of His magnificent love, and in every one of His blessings to each of us, God is showing how much he loves us individually.

I know <u>I'm being long winded</u>, but <u>I don't know how</u> to express God's depth of love that <u>He really does have</u> for each one of us, and it is holy, honorable, peaceful, personal, real, pure, righteous and dignified. And His love is full and free and all we ever need because it is His presence. It is Himself.

The ultimate joy of God and His people and the ultimate salvation, is the <u>newness of the new world</u> as said the prophet Isaiah. He referred to Knowledge of God as the ...

ULTIMATE UTOPIA

"They shall not hurt nor destroy in all my holy mountain: for the earth shall be full of the knowledge of the LORD, as the waters cover the sea."

Isaiah 11:9

When one is filled with **Knowledge of God** then nothing holds its own attraction but instead speaks of God's goodness, exalts God, and draws all people always nearer to God, all the time.

This also puts **meaning** in our lives. When this is effectual, nothing is without **meaning**. Then everything has exceeding depth of meaning. This is because we realize that everything's very existence is <u>for the purpose of speaking about our loving God</u>. Everything shows and teaches us about our God. This also gives everything infinite purpose, and the highest and most ultimate purpose. Then life and everything in life becomes **meaningful**, a <u>dramatic</u> and exciting adventure. **What could be more <u>dramatic</u> and adventurous than getting to know an all-powerful, all-loving God that holds everything in the palm of His hand, created everything, is everywhere, loves us beyond measure, and beyond the limits of our imagination?** This is possible because Jesus poured out his blood for us on the cross. Anyone who <u>trusts in God</u> becomes **instantly perfect**.

"At what instant I shall speak concerning a nation, and concerning a kingdom, to pluck up, and to pull down, and to destroy it; If that nation, against whom I have spoken, turn from their evil, I will repent of the evil that I thought to do to them. And at what instant I shall speak concerning a nation, and concerning a kingdom, to build and to plant it; If it do evil in my sight, that it obey not my voice, then I will repent of the good, with which I said I would benefit them.

Jer. 18:7-10

*When I shall say to
the righteous, that, he
shall surely live; if he trust to his
own righteousness, and commit
iniquity, all his righteousnesses shall
not be remembered, but for his iniquity
that he has committed, he shall die for
it. Again, when I say to the wicked,
You shall surely die;
if he turn from his sin, and do that
which is lawful and right; If the
wicked restore . . . None of his sins that
he has committed shall be
mentioned to him..."*

Ezekiel 33:13-16

Jesus' blood makes it possible for any nation or individual to turn to God and <u>instantly</u> have a "clean slate", with all mistakes and sins <u>forgotten by God</u>. God will say, **"It never happened."** concerning the wrongs that have been committed. If anyone continually turns to God, then he has a <u>brand new life all the time</u>. I know that is why Jesus poured out His blood on the cross. Some people think it's gory and gruesome, and may call it, "a bloody religion." But it was <u>God's passion</u> to demonstrate in a real, tangible way, the depth of His love for us. He truly *desired* to pour out His blood for us. It came from the <u>depths of His heart</u>. It came from His yearning to show us how much He loves us.

He *greatly desired* to do it. When Jesus had communion with His disciples at the Last Supper He exclaimed,

With desire I have desired to eat this Passover meal with you before I suffer . . .

"For I say to you, I will not anymore eat of it, until it be fulfilled in the kingdom of God. And he took the cup, and gave thanks, and said, Take this, and divide it among yourselves: For I say to you, I will not drink of the fruit of the vine, until the kingdom of God shall come. And he took bread, and gave thanks, and broke it, and gave to them, saying, This is my body which is given for you: this do in remembrance of me. Likewise also the cup after supper, saying, This cup is the new testament in my blood, which is shed for you." (Luke 22:15-20).

I would like to speak at length about the blood of Jesus and what it means because with *"With desire..."* He *"desired..."* to give His blood for us.

The pouring out of Jesus' blood was the answer for God's people to many years of yearning after His righteousness. Since the beginning, when mankind first turned away from God and brought the curse of death, sickness, every other evil, and eternal death into the world, God has had a blood covenant with man. God declares "**...the blood is the life:**" (Deuteronomy 12:23). "**For the life of the flesh is in the blood : and I have given it to you upon the altar to make an atonement for your souls: for it is the blood that makes an atonement for the soul...For it is the life of all flesh; the blood of it is for the life of it: therefore I said to the children of Israel, You shall eat the blood of no manner of flesh: for the life of all flesh is the blood of it:**" (Leviticus 17:11,15), and in Hebrews 9:22, "**without the shedding of blood there is no remission." So when Jesus gave us His blood, God gave us His life.**

When mankind first turned away from God through Adam and Eve, they tried to cover themselves with fig leaves and hide from God because for the first time they knew they were naked. They had chosen knowledge of self

over **Knowledge of God**, and lust instead of trust. **God killed some animals, pouring out the first animal blood. This blood sacrifice by God** was to cover Adam and Eve's nakedness. Adam's son **Able, also shed animal blood** when he gave God an acceptable sacrifice, killing a lamb. But God didn't accept his brother Cain's sacrifice, the works of his hands. God said to him, **"If you do well, won't you be accepted?"** (Genesis 4:7). That is why Cain killed Able, because God approved of his brother's sacrifice, but not his. **Noah also shed animal blood** when he offered a thanksgiving sacrifice to God after the great flood and **"the LORD smelled a sweet savor."** (Genesis 7:21). **Abraham, shed animal blood** when by God's instructions he killed animals for a sacrifice, when God made an eternal oath with him (Genesis 15: 8-21). When God delivered His people out of the hands of Pharaoh king of Egypt, the final plague was that the haters of God would lose their firstborn sons and the firstborn of their cattle. **God told Moses**, each family that feared Him must **kill a lamb and put some of its blood on the doorpost:**

"and when I see the blood,
I will pass over you . . ."
Exodus 12:13

Moses also was given intricate detailed instruction from God, about how the children of Israel should offer acceptable sacrifices on His altar, so the <u>animal blood would cover their sins</u>. When Jesus came, he was to give the final blood sacrifice for all time. All the other sacrifices were a picture of what God had been planning to do even before the creation of the world, for the redemption of mankind, in the pouring out of <u>His own blood</u>. Jesus said <u>he came into the world to die!!!</u>

"Even as the Son of man came not
to be ministered to, but to minister, and
to give his life as a ransom for many."
Matthew 2:28

After Jesus poured out his own blood, there would never be a need for another animal sacrifice ! The Bible teaches us that the animal sacrifices <u>covered sin</u>, but

Jesus' blood <u>**took away**</u> all mankind's sins,
<u>**once and for all**</u>, for all time.

So those perfected by the blood of Jesus should have "**no more consciousness of sins.**" (Hebrews 10: 2). That is <u>why</u> Jesus **wanted** to pour out his blood. He **wanted** to give that:

<u>*Eternal Perfect Gift*</u> *to all mankind.*

<u>*He wanted us to have peace with God*</u>

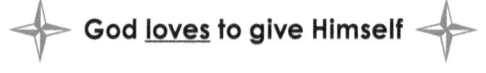

"For if the blood of bulls and of goats, . . . sprinkling the unclean, sanctified to the purifying of the flesh: How much more shall the blood of Christ, who through the eternal Spirit offered himself without spot to God, purge your conscience from dead works to serve the living God?... Nor yet that he should offer himself often... For then he must have often have suffered since the foundation of the world: but now once in the end of the world he has appeared to put away sin by the sacrifice of himself."

"Then I said,

Look, I come

(in the volume of the book it is written

of me) to do your will, Oh God . . .

He takes away the first, that he

may establish the second. By the

which will we are sanctified through

the offering of the body of

Jesus Christ once for all . . .

For by one offering he has perfected

forever them that are sanctified."

Hebrews 9:13,14,25,26

10:7,9,10,14

When Jesus said, "I go to prepare a place for you," He really meant it, of course.

Since God poured out His blood for us, you can be sure God will pour out His best of **EVERYTHING** else: "how shall he not with him also freely give us all things?" (Romans 8:32). And since He is all knowing, He knows what he can give to make us especially happy and comfort us individually. And as a loving Father He takes delight in doing so! That's why in Isaiah God says, " Then shall the lambs feed after their manner." (Isaiah 5:17), and "...flocks, which shall lie down, and none shall make them afraid." (Isaiah 17:2). Each one of us has different personalities, potentials, likes, dislikes, and particular things that we really enjoy, even if they mean nothing to anyone else. God understands this, really cares, and <u>really</u> wants to make each one of us happy according to our <u>own</u> preferences, endeavors, personalities, aspirations and desires.

God's blessings are custom made!!!

As we get to know God more and feel closer to Him, we will feel more secure and relaxed because His person is real, warm, friendly, and comforting. He gives the ultimate sense of security because He is real security.

When God is our life and we are filled with **Knowledge of God** it makes us indestructible, because He is indestructible. It makes us eternal, because He is eternal. It makes us pure, because He is pure. It makes us perfect, because He is perfect. It makes us always brand new, because He is always brand new. It makes us beautiful, because He is beautiful. It makes us without darkness or a doubt, because He is without darkness or a doubt. It makes us without confusion, because He is without confusion. It makes us without failure, because He is without failure. It makes us without sin, because He is without sin. **Knowledge of God** allows us to *escape* our own minds, shortcomings, thoughts, and viewpoints. It lifts us up to a higher level, His level, where He is, with Him, in Him and one with Him.

We can walk in newness of life all the time. God is real and we are real, and if we choose to fill our minds with **Knowledge of God** instead of knowledge of ourselves, then we have left our own lives behind and our own sense of existence, and in truth, we no longer exist except in the knowledge, presence, and person of God.

A human being needs to have some kind of attention to have a sense of existence, because the very essence of existing, and being human is to be aware of one's self. But if one chooses never to think about one's self and chooses rather to think only about God, then he loses his own sense of being and existence, and no longer has a sense of self. Having no sense of self leaves only the knowledge and sense of God's

Beautiful gorgeous being!!

If one chooses never to think of another person's being but rather God's being, that is, to think of God manifested in the lives of others, then one has ceased to give others <u>any</u> sense of being and existence apart from God. One instead sees God's existence and person in others. This is realizing the presence of God. This is recognizing and acknowledging God as the <u>only</u> true person who really exists. God indeed <u>is</u> the only true person who is manifested in and through us. God becomes our life as we see **Knowledge of God** in other people. When we realize this, no <u>other person exists</u> in our lives except God, that is, when we <u>refuse</u> to acknowledge another person's existence apart from God and instead, we <u>acknowledge God's person</u> in them. As it is written: "**God accepts no man's person...**" (Galatians 2:6) **"will he be pleased with you, or accept your person?"** (Malachi 1:8) **"See, you are of nothing, and your work of nothing: an abomination <u>is he that</u> chooses you."** (Isaiah 41:24). And God says in Malachi 1:9,

"will he regard your persons?"

"...because of false brethren unawares brought in, who came in secretly to spy out our liberty which we have in Christ Jesus, that they might bring us into bondage: To whom we gave place by subjection, no, not for an hour; that the truth of the gospel might continue with you. But of these who seemed to be somewhat, (whatever they were, it doesn't matter to me: God accepts no man's person;) for they who seemed to be somewhat in agreement added nothing to me."

Galatians 2:5,6

Personal Notes, Thoughts

THIS DOESN'T RUIN LIFE.

On the contrary, this gives true life to each of us and stops all criticism we have one towards another because if God is all, and in all, **as it is written** in Scripture:

Christ is all, and in all."

Colossians 3:11

we can't criticize each other without criticizing God. Then we have no knowledge of each other, but only Knowledge of God, the one true God.

"But God forbid that I should glory, except in the cross of our Lord Jesus Christ, By whom the world is crucified to me, and I to the world."

Galatians 6:14

This lifts people up and does not put them down. To acknowledge God in them will give life to them, not take life away from them, for God is life. They will shine more brilliantly than ever, and their own being will flourish more and more. They will be healthier and stronger on account of our seeing God in them. This is because God is among us and in us! For those who **choose God**, **God is glorified in all and through all, and lives in all and through all. In turn we all give all glory only to God, and worship only Him, forever. Amen.**

Integration of Prayer into Knowledge of God, Ponderings

When I wait on Jesus, the Lord God, I like to imagine myself millions of years from now still waiting, waiting, waiting. I sincerely enjoy this. I feel like a baby in its mother's womb. It is peaceful and secure. At times I can sense God moving in part of my mind, spirit or emotions. True rest comes just in knowing that God is there, and there forever, and that I am trusting myself to Him. Sometimes I feel Him changing me. Sometimes I don't. But I don't worry because I know He's there taking care of me and watching over me.

I have the assurance that I am His and He is mine. I know that He's there and He will take care of me. Then I can know God in such a deeper way. Gaining **Knowledge of God** in this way doesn't depend on the senses, but its just knowing that He's there, and He is watching over me, and that the Almighty is using His power to minister to me in any way that I need. He also ministers to me in ways that I don't know that I need.

Integration of Prayer into Knowledge of God

When I am still and quiet before Him I have no sense of time, just a sense that God is eternal and that He will take care of me forever. I wait, and wait, and wait, for Him to give me something to say to Him that comes from my heart, not out of a sense of duty or saying what's right, not a formula or a word of tension, fear, obligation and such like. I really want to say something from my heart, without fear, out of a quiet, peaceful, and restful feeling. So if I don't get any words in my mind that are peaceful, restful and genuine, I just don't say anything. Then I can rest in God, in **Knowledge of God**.

I don't speak unless words enter my mind that come from a deep inner peace instilled by childlike trust from the Holy Spirit. He seems to give me an ability to respond to Him in trust slowly, drop by drop. I may wait for hours and hours and hours and say nothing at all. God's love and presence enfolds me and releases me from all darkness. He removes and sets me free from many burdens, mind-sets and ways of thinking that may be damaging to myself or others, or unexplainable things that may have taken

hold on me. Sometimes I feel that our Heavenly Father is helping me to open up to Him from deep within, in ways I don't understand, and sometimes I feel very close to Him face to face, eyes to eyes. It's just like I'm staring at Him and He at me and that my eyes are fixed on the God of the universe and His on mine. I really like and really love this feeling. It makes me feel so secure, that I want to stay there forever. I guess it must be sort of like a baby sucking on its mother's breast. Care may not vanish immediately, and sometimes I may become troubled, my mind may wander, or I may get disturbing thoughts. If this happens, I just say my little prayer again:

Dear Heavenly Father,
I ask that you would give me something to say to you,
from a heart of trust.
I ask that I would wait for you forever.
In Jesus' name I pray.
Amen.

And we grow in Knowledge of God as we wait on Him.

Integration of Prayer into Knowledge of God

When I lived in Fairbanks, Alaska, I think it was in 1982, I had permission from my Pastor, Juanita, to remain at our small church to pray. Rosanne, my only child at that time, was about two years old. My Christian girlfriend who had three children of her own, cared for my daughter as I remained in prayer at church, at the altar, for about three days with no activity or food.

During this time, periodically I would have disturbing thoughts. Words came into my mind from God, "Just let them pass through." So I followed that advice, and just continued to wait on the LORD, there at the altar. All disturbing thoughts <u>did</u> "just pass through." Then it was as if they had never been, and God gave me a deep peace and inner comfort.

Also during this time while waiting at the altar, the thought came to me from God, "If you think words, it is like wet cement. If you speak them out, it is like dried cement." That helped me to understand the importance and power of my words as I waited there alone with God.

Integration of Prayer into Knowledge of God

I chose exactly which words to leave as thought in my mind, and which words to speak out.

When I got a few words in my mind that were genuine and real, and truly came from an honest, peaceful, trusting heart, I spoke them out to God, my Savior Jesus Christ. None of my words though, were necessarily earth shaking, or of any exceptional insight, or deep rooted wisdom, but just honest and real. Usually they were simple and insignificant, but they were real, true, and peaceful.

I began to feel a peaceful warmth in various parts of my brain. Sometimes it would begin in my head, and spread to another part of my body. When this happened, it usually increased, until I was quite warm in whatever part of my body the warmth was spreading. It was a little strange, but peaceful and comforting. It interested me and was amazing to me, that God was moving in me.

Integration of Prayer into Knowledge of God

My Pastor Juanita walked in once, for a couple minutes, and said excitedly, "You are so hot!" and then put her hand on my chest and continued, "Have you been dancing, jumping around, or singing?" "No," I said, "Just waiting at the altar." As she walked out she said emphatically, "Pray for me!"

By waiting quietly before God **I can hopefully learn to choose my words carefully, not only in prayer, but at <u>all times</u>**. For all of us, waiting quietly before God, whether it be in our own private "prayer chambers", living rooms, or anywhere, choosing our words carefully in prayer will hopefully spill into our everyday lives. As it is written, God creates the fruit of the lips:

> "I create the fruit of the lips;
> Peace, peace to him that is far off,
> and to him that is near,
> says the LORD,
> and I will heal him."
> Isaiah 57:19

God speaks of the great dangers of our tongues:

Even so the tongue is a little member, and boasts great things. See, how great a matter a little fire kindles! And the tongue is a fire, a world of iniquity: so is the tongue among our members, that it defiles the whole body, and sets on fire the course of nature; and it is set on fire of hell. For every kind of beast, and of bird, and of snake, and of things in the sea, is tamed, and has been tamed of mankind: But the tongue can no man tame; it is an unruly evil, full of deadly poison. With it we bless God, even the Father; and with it we curse men, which are made after the similitude of God. Out of the same mouth proceeds blessing and cursing. My brothers and sisters, these things ought not to be. Does a fountain send forth at the same place sweet water and bitter? Can the fig tree, my bothers and sisters, bear olive berries? Either a vine, figs? So can no fountain give both salt water and fresh." (James 3:5-13).

IF ANY MAN CAN CONTROL HIS TONGUE HE IS PERFECT

"If any man offends not
in word,
the same is a perfect man,
and able also to bridle
the whole body.
See, we put bits in the horses' mouths,
that they may obey us; and we turn
about their whole body.
See also the ships,
which though they be so great, and
are driven by fierce winds, yet they are
turned about with a very small helm,
wherever the commander wishes."

James 3:2-4

"For with stammering lips
and another tongue
will he speak to this people.
To whom he said, This is the rest
with which you may cause the weary
to rest; and this is the refreshing: yet
they would not hear... For thus says
the LORD GOD,
the Holy One of Israel; In returning
and rest you shall be saved: in
quietness and confidence shall be your
strength: and you wouldn't.
But you said, No..."
Isaiah 28:11,12 30:15,16

Personal Notes, Thoughts

Over the years I have <u>neglected</u> to spend ample time waiting quietly on God. However lately, I have begun again to understand how important and vital it is.

Old Testament prophesy in the previous Bible verse is referring to the Holy Spirit's gift of speaking in "tongues", yet another way to gain **Knowledge of God**.

I speak in "tongues" by faith. That is, I feel nothing. Some people feel something. I have not and do not. I began to speak in "tongues" out of trust and as an act of faith, after many years of seeking unsuccessfully, to "receive" the gift of "tongues". It is written of in 1 Corinthians chapters 12 and 14:

"Now there are diversities of gifts, but the same Spirit. And there are differences of administrations, but the same Lord. And there are varieties of operations, but is the same God which works all in all. But the manifestation of the Spirit is given to every man with which to profit. For to one is given by the Spirit the word of wisdom; to another the word of knowledge by the same Spirit; to another faith

by the same Spirit to another the gifts of healing by the same Spirit; to another the working of miracles; to another prophecy; to another discerning of spirits; to another <u>different</u> kinds of tongues; But all these are worked by the one and the same Spirit, distributing to every man as he wishes... (12: 4-11).

Follow after pure love, and desire spiritual gifts, but rather that you may prophesy. For he that speaks in an <u>unknown</u> tongue speaks not to men, but to God: for no man understands <u>him</u>; nevertheless in the spirit he speaks mysteries. But he that prophesies speaks to men to edification and exhortation, and comfort. He that speaks in an <u>unknown</u> tongue edifies himself; but he that prophesies edifies the church. I wish that you all spoke with tongues, but rather that you prophesied: for greater is he that prophesies than he that speaks with tongues, except he interpret, that the church may receive edifying. (14:1-5).

Therefore let him that speaks in an <u>unknown</u> tongue pray that he may interpret. For if I pray in an <u>unknown</u> tongue, my spirit prays, but my understanding is unfruitful. What will I do? I will pray with the spirit, and I will pray with the understanding also: I will sing with the spirit, and I will sing with the understanding also. (14:13-15).

I thank my God, I speak with tongues more than all of you: Yet in the church I would rather speak five words with my understanding, that <u>by my voice</u> I may teach others also, than ten thousand words in an <u>unknown</u> tongue. Brothers and sisters, be not children in understanding: although in malice be children, but in understanding be men. In the law it is written, with <u>men of</u> other tongues and other lips I will speak to this people; and yet for all that they will not hear me, says the LORD." (14:18-21).

Therefore, my brothers and sisters, covet to prophesy and forbid not to speak with tongues." (14: 39-40).

Integration of Prayer into Knowledge of God

I like to pray in "tongues". I like to pray and pray and wait for God to move in my heart. I like to expect the Holy Spirit to move in my heart as I pray in "tongues". I also like to join in prayer with others, and for others, especially if someone is "being ministered to" at church. In such cases I feel a deep desire for God to move by the power of His Holy Spirit, to set that person free from anything that may be bothering them such as cares, bondages, sicknesses, or other problems.

Then my heart yearns for them to receive benefit through prayer, that they may be <u>touched by God</u>. I want God to meet all their needs. I realize that nothing is hard for God. Everything is easy for Him. And God has given us the avenue of prayer as a means to help others, and the gift of "tongues".

When others are around and also are praying, it gives me great stamina and energy to continue, and to not give up until the Lord has ministered to an individual. Sometimes it seems to take a lot of stamina and fortitude to continue. All by myself I seem to "peter out" before persisting to see

a certain person receive a blessing, or an answer from the LORD. But I have extreme confidence in God's desire to supernaturally help those that are in need of Him, or need something specific from God. Some people are crying out in their hearts for help, and <u>appreciate</u> prayer and are deeply thankful for it.

Increasing in the <u>Knowledge of God</u> is possible through our own prayer life, and in time we spend alone waiting quietly on Him. He wants us to reach out to others in prayer, and also in tangible ways, to meet their natural needs. We know that through prayer, all addictions can be broken, needs met, heavy burdens lifted, Satanic strongholds dissolved, and genetics carrying evil or destructive messages in the DNA and chromosomes regenerated through creative miracles, from our dear, loving, caring, and compassionate Heavenly Father.

Dear Heavenly Father,

I ask that you would give me

something to say to you,

from a heart of trust.

I ask that I would wait for you forever.

In Jesus' name I pray.

Amen.

Conclusion

Conclusion

Conclusion to Knowledge of God, Ponderings

Knowledge of God must be married to **Trust in God** to be effectual and fruitful. One cannot survive without the other. **Knowledge of God** without trust allows no flow of God into us and out of us. Trust on the other hand without **Knowledge of God** allows no place on which trust can rest, to obtain the life of God, the real God, the Creator of everything.

When **Knowledge of God** and **Trust in God** are hand-in-hand, married, coexistent, coactive and one, each fully alive and well, a beautiful life of God can flow richly into our lives. He will be healing us, blessing us, and giving us peace and rest. God's life will be bringing in the new world with full deliverance from all darkness, that new world, world without end. There will be no sickness, pain, death, sorrow, confusion, broken hearts, being separated from loved ones, misunderstandings, lack of comprehension, heavy bondages, crosses to bear, or oppression. There will only be rejoicing in our loving God, and He in us, forever.

"But Israel

shall be saved

in the LORD

with an everlasting salvation:

you shall not be ashamed

or confounded,

world without end."

Isaiah 45:17

Also, in continually building on Knowledge of God to which we have attained, prayer is essential:

> *Jesus said,*
> *"Is it not written,*
> *My house shall be called of all nations*
> *the house of prayer?"*
> *Mark 11:17*

Our bodies are His house, not just a church building, as spoken of in 1 Corinthians 3:16, "Don't you know that you are the temple of God, and <u>that</u> the Spirit of God lives in you?" In the next Scriptures our Heavenly Father not only speaks of His house being a house of prayer, but also declares:

1) **Keep silence before me, let the people come near, then let them speak.**
2) **Bind up the testimony, seal the law among my disciples.**
3) **Should not the people seek their God? <u>The living to the dead?</u>**
4) **If they do not speak according to this word, it is because <u>there is no light in them.</u>**

*"Even them I will

bring to my holy mountain,

and make them joyful in

my house of prayer:

their burnt offerings

and their sacrifices <u>shall be</u> accepted on

my altar; for my house shall be called a

house of prayer

for all people."*

Isaiah 56:7

"Keep silence before me,

Oh islands;

and let the people renew <u>their</u>

strength:

let them come near; then let them speak;

let us come near together

to judgment."

Isaiah 41:1

"Bind up the testimony,
seal the law among my disciples.
And I will wait
on the LORD, that hides his face
from the house of Jacob, and I will look
for him. See, I and the children
whom the LORD has given me
are for signs and for wonders in Israel
from the LORD of hosts,
who lives in mount Zion...
should not a people seek to their God?
for the living to the dead?
To the law and to the testimony:
if they do not speak according to this word,
it is because there is no light in them."
Isaiah 8:16-20

True waiting on God brings zealous works of God that **LOOSEN** bondages, **REMOVE** heavy yokes, **FREE** God's children from destructive habits, **BREAK** all the works of the enemy, and **RELEASE** them from harmful ways of thinking and all darkness.

God delivers a message to His sorely disappointed people, in Isaiah chapter 58, who have been trying to seek Him, but somehow completely misunderstood God's true desires and intentions: "Is it such a fast that I have chosen? A day for a man to afflict his soul? Is it to bow down his head as a bulrush, and to spread sackcloth and ashes under him? Will you call this a fast, and an acceptable day to the LORD?

Is not this the fast that I have chosen? To loose the bands of wickedness, to undo the heavy burdens, to let the oppressed go free, and that you break every yoke? Is it not to deal your bread to the hungry and that you bring the poor that are cast out into your house? When you see the naked that you cover him and that you hide not yourself from your own flesh?

Conclusion

Then shall your light break forth as the morning, and your health shall spring forth speedily: and your righteousness shall go before you; the glory of the LORD shall be your rear guard. Then you shall call and the LORD shall answer; you shall cry, and he shall say Here I <u>am</u>, If you take away from the midst of you the yoke, the putting forth of the finger, and speaking vanity; And <u>if</u> you draw out your soul to the hungry, and satisfy the afflicted soul, then shall your light rise in obscurity, and your darkness <u>be</u> as the noon day: And the LORD shall guide you continually and satisfy your soul in drought, and make fat your bones: and you shall be like a watered garden, and like a spring of water, whose waters do not fail.

And they <u>that shall be</u> of thee shall build the old waste places: you shall raise up the foundations of many generations; and you shall be called The repairer of the breach, The restorer of paths to live in.

If you turn away your foot from the *Sabbath*, <u>from</u> doing your pleasure on my holy day; and call the *Sabbath* a delight, the holy of the LORD, honorable; and shall honor him, not doing your own ways, nor finding <u>your own</u> pleasure, nor speaking your own words.

Then you shall delight yourself in the LORD, and I will cause you to ride upon the high places of the earth, and feed you with the heritage of Jacob your father for the mouth of the LORD has spoken it."

Isaiah 5:5-14

Conclusion

In that chapter, God directs prayer to a specific end, introducing the chapter, Isaiah 58, by trumpeting His voice through the Holy Spirit, to His own, struggling, desperate, ineffectual, outwardly devout people saying: "Cry aloud, and spare not, lift up your voice like a trumpet and show my people their transgression and the house of Jacob their sin. Yet they seek me daily, and delight to know my ways as a nation that did righteousness, and forsook not the ordinances of their God; they ask of me the ordinances of justice, they take delight in approaching to God. "

The people had been fasting and seeking God. But true waiting on God brings the works of God through us by His Holy Spirit and His Holy Spirit's inspiration.

Getting quiet before God allows the Almighty to conquer enemies that we cannot conquer, enemies that attack us from within or from without. God is bigger and stronger than they are, whoever or whatever they are, however they come, and wherever they come from. It doesn't

matter whether they are too strong for us, God is always stronger and knows how to destroy His enemies, those enemies of his children. In Isaiah God speaks to His enemies, "you, <u>are</u> dissolved..." (14:31), says of them, "they are extinct..." (43:17), that "<u>They are</u> dead, they shall not live; <u>they are</u> deceased..." and "He has made all their memory to perish." (26:14). In Psalm 18:17,

*King David said,
"He delivered me from my strong
enemy, and from them that hated me
for they were too strong for me."*

As we wait quietly before God, He takes up our battle, and fights the warfare that wars against our soul. Waiting on God forms a relationship with Him. Our inner core can form a great dependency on God. This is wonderful. We can learn to belong to the one we were <u>*really*</u> meant to belong to, <u>*our LORD Jesus Christ*</u>.

Jesus protected his disciples from all evil through the power of God's name. He prayed before he died: "While I was with them in the world, I kept them in your name: those that you gave me I have kept, and none of them is lost, but the son of perdition; that the scripture would be fulfilled." (John 17: 12).

In the earliest hours of the morning, during later hours at night, or in the midnight hours when all is quiet, I love to lie still and pray my little prayer to God ♥ and wait on Him...

Dear Heavenly Father,
I ask that you would give me something to say to you,
from a heart of trust.
I ask that I would wait for you forever.
In Jesus' name I pray.
Amen.

<u>Summary to Knowledge of God, Ponderings</u>

All of life comes from God. We love Him dearly if we know Him. And He desires to know us if we do not know Him.

He is the giver of, and answer to all of life. When we find Him, we can rejoice in Him. When we know Him, we can rest in Him. **May God's glories fall on all of us. May He fulfill His will in all of us**. May all His desires for <u>His</u> new world come to pass in us and through us.

As we get to know our loving God, our loving Heavenly Father, **more and more**, we will be able to rest in Him <u>**more and more**</u>. He will delight to unveil His wondrous mysteries hidden from the foundations of the world. He will give to us and be to us <u>**much more**</u> than we have ever **imagined or dreamt!**

And when he
(Jesus) was
demanded of the Pharisees,
when the kingdom of God should
come, he answered them and said,
The kingdom of God does
Not come with observation:
Neither shall they say,
Look here! Or, look there!

for, consider this,
the kingdom of God is within you."

Luke 17:20-21

"For unto us a child is born, unto us a son is given: and the government shall be upon his shoulder: and his name shall be called Wonderful, Counselor, The mighty God, The everlasting Father, The Prince of Peace. Of the increase of his government and peace there shall be no end, upon the throne of David, and upon his kingdom, to order it, and to establish it with judgment and with justice from now on even forever. The zeal of the LORD of hosts will perform this."

Isaiah 9: 6-7

The LORD of hosts has sworn, saying, Surely as I have thought, _so_ shall it come to pass; and as I have purposed, so shall it stand: . . . then shall his yoke depart from off them, and his burden depart from off their shoulders. This _is_ the purpose that is purposed upon the whole earth: and this _is_ the hand that is stretched out upon all the nations. For the LORD of hosts has purposed, and who shall disannul _it_? and his hand _is_ stretched out, and who shall turn it back?"

Isaiah 14:24-27

"And in this mountain
shall the LORD of hosts
make unto all people
a feast of fat things, a feast of
wines on the lees,
of fat things full of marrow, of
wines on the lees
well refined. And he will destroy
in this mountain
the face of the covering cast over
all people,
and the vail that is spread over
all nations.
He will swallow up death in victory;

and the Lord GOD will
wipe away tears from off all faces;
and the rebuke of his people shall he
take away from off all the earth :
for the LORD has spoken it.
And it shall be said in that day,
Look, this is our God; we have waited
for him, and he will save us: this is the
LORD; we have waited for him,
we will be glad
and rejoice in his salvation.
For in this mountain shall the hand
of the LORD rest, . . . "

Isaiah 25:6-10

Personal Notes, Thoughts

"Open the gates,
that the righteous nation which keeps the truth may enter in.
You will keep him in perfect peace, whose mind is fixed
on you because he trusts in you. Trust in the LORD
forever: for in the LORD JEHOVA
is everlasting strength:"
Isaiah 26:2-4

"I did not say to the seed of Jacob, Seek me in vain: I the
LORD speak righteousness, I declare things that are right."
Isaiah 45:19

 *Trust in God*

"And they brought
to him also infants, that he would touch them: but when his
disciples saw it, they refused them. But Jesus called them
to him, and said, Permit little children to come to me, and
forbid them not: for of such is the kingdom of God.
Truly I say to you, Whoever shall not
receive the kingdom of God
as a little child shall in
no way enter in."
Luke 18:15-17

"him that comes to me I will in no way cast out."

Introduction to Trust in God

Introduction to Trust in God, Ponderings

Trust in God is beautiful, simple, free, childlike; a release from all – sin – darkness – evil – wickedness – deceit – deception – manipulation – falsehood – fakery – imitation – It is not imitation, because it is the real life of God. God doesn't have to imitate anyone.

The Bible teaches, "That we should be to the praise of his glory, who first trusted in Christ. In whom you also trusted, after that you heard the word of truth, the gospel (good news) of your salvation: in whom also after that you believed, you were sealed with that holy Spirit of promise." (Ephesians 1:12-13).

Trust releases the glory of **GOD**. There is no lust in trust. There is no trying in trust. There is no trying to be better in trust. Trust is letting **GOD** be good in us, not us trying to be good. **Trust in God** is the ultimate valve that releases **GOD** into us. **Trust in God** opens up the heavens into an ever-unfolding and

unveiling of GOD, into an ever-increasing adventure of His glory, love, majesty, majestic beauty and all the goodness that flows from GOD.

Scripture teaches,

"Every good gift

and perfect gift

is from above,

and comes down

from the Father of lights,

with whom is no variableness

neither shadow of turning"

James 1:17

Trust in God, Ponderings

Why did God choose **Trust in God** to unveil His mysteries?

- **Because it leaves no one out * * ***
- **Because it leaves no ingredient of man * * ***

If there is an ingredient of man, it puts poison in the food and it becomes deadly. Why does it become deadly?

Because God is life, and all life and creation is an expression of Himself, no one else. If there is any ingredient of man it puts **SOMEONE ELSE NEXT TO GOD**, but God did not invite us to be next to Him, but to be **ONE WITH HIM!**

Satan invited Adam and Eve to be next to God, to be like God, to raise themselves to His level by gaining His wisdom. But on the other hand, God had provided the

tree of life, *Christ Himself.* This would have meant oneness with God, because Jesus said, "I am the way, the truth, and the life..."

If they had chosen to eat of the tree of life, to *embrace truth*, God Himself, they would have had <u>*koinonia* (Greek) *{communion, intimacy and marriage} with God*</u>. But I guess they were bored with it, didn't give it a second thought, didn't care. Oh well, <u>I guess they wanted the **curse on the earth** instead</u>. Becoming one with God is a beautiful and awesome invitation: To actually have the privilege and honor of being perfectly one with Him who created everything and is all-powerful and all-loving. We have been invited to be one, perfectly one in His holy communion with His own wife, His precious Holy Spirit and be one in their marital intimacies. This is holy and sacred. It is not defiled because we become one with God. However, if we try to be like Him, instead of one with Him, we defile ourselves and His people, and become detestable and vulgar, because it is intimacy without holy matrimony.

That they all may be one as you, Father, are in me, and I in you, that they also may be one in us : that the world may believe that you have sent me. And the glory which you gave me I have given them; that they may be one, even as we are one: I in them, and you in me, that they may be made perfect in one; and that the world may know that you have sent me, and have loved them, as you have loved me."

John 17:21-23

Personal Notes, Thoughts

So **Trust in God** brings the oneness with God that Jesus prayed for to his Heavenly Father, for us. It cannot come through effort of any kind, because it is the opposite of effort, letting God be God, letting God be big in us, like a little baby in his Father's arms. Infants were brought to Jesus. They did not yet know how to talk, walk, or crawl, but perhaps could sit and look around. This was Jesus' response:

> "And they brought to him also infants, that he would touch them . . . 'Truly I say to you, Whoever shall not receive the kingdom of God as a little child shall in no way enter in.'"
> Luke 18:17

Jesus was setting forth a perfect example of trust. Trust in God allows God to get all glory, because if we are doing <u>nothing</u>, then God is doing everything, and if God is doing everything, then <u>there is nothing for which we can take credit</u>.

So Trust in God is the ultimate, because it brings the ultimate glory of God. When God alone is glorified, then God will show up. That is, He will flow freely and hold nothing back of His glory and wonders. One of God's names in the Bible in the Old Testament is <u>Jealous</u>, "For thou shalt worship no other god: for the LORD, whose name <u>is</u> Jealous, <u>is</u> a jealous God:" (Exodus 34:14), showing that God refuses to share His glory with another. In the book of Isaiah God says,

I will not give my glory to another."

Isaiah 48:11

God refuses to be in competition with anyone.

God is a majority all by Himself.

God says at the end of the exhausting book of Ezekiel in chapter 43, verse 9, "Now let them put away their whoredom, and the carcasses of their kings far from me, and I will live among them forever." God's opinion of us trying to be like Him, to share or get some of His glory, is like a bunch of dead carcasses, <u>not</u> a pretty picture. The Apostle Paul, who wrote two thirds of the New Testament, described his own struggle against evil that he found in himself: "Oh wretched man that I am; Who shall deliver me from the body of this death?" (Romans 7: 24).

So until we <u>desert</u> self effort we will never have peace and rest in God. God says, **"I will hide my face from them, I will see what their end <u>shall be</u>: for they <u>are</u> a very froward generation, children in whom <u>is</u> no faith."** (Deuteronomy 32:20). This is also what God was referring to when He said,

> *"Perfect peace has he whose*
> *mind is fixed on you*
> *because he trusts in you."*
> *(Isaiah 26: 3).*

The verse jut cited was introduced by s the following verse:

"Open the gates that the righteous nation which keeps the truth may enter in."
Isaiah 26:2

This is that <u>truth</u> to which God was referring. The very statement that is <u>on our money here in the United States of America</u>, "In God we trust," is eternal truth. **Trust in God** is the true foundation of eternal security, stability and strength for any nation or individual person.

We will find great favor with God as we exalt the truth of God's grace, and do not forsake this simple truth, **Trust in God**.

When Jesus told Peter, **"Your name is Peter and upon this rock I shall build my church and the gates of hell shall not prevail against it,"** he was <u>simply responding to Peter's true acknowledgement of who he really was</u>, not to anything Peter had done. Peter had just said,

> *You are the Christ,*
> *the son of the living God."*
> *Matthew 16:16*

When Peter began to speak of his own opinions later on, Jesus did not acknowledge Peter. Jesus instead <u>addressed Satan, while still conversing with Peter</u>. He said, **"Get behind me, Satan: you are an offense to me: for you savor not the things that be of God, but those that be of men."** When Peter had used his mouth, mind, and heart to exalt God then he became a conduit of God, a vessel of God. Jesus could lift up Peter because Peter was lifting Him up.

The human element was not getting in the way.

As long as we look in ourselves we are in sin.

Jesus said…

"Truly, truly, I say to you, whoever commits sin is the servant of sin. And the servant does not live in the house forever: but the Son lives forever. It the Son therefore shall make you free, you shall be free indeed."

Jesus also said:

"For whoever will

save his life

shall lose it;

but whoever shall lose his life

for my sake and the gospel's,

the same shall save it.

For what shall it profit a man, if

he gains the whole world, and loses his

own soul? Or what shall a man give in

exchange for his soul?"

Mark 8:35-37

Personal Notes, Thoughts

If we are willing to forsake ourselves for God, and exchange trust in ourselves (or someone else for that matter because mankind is one), for **Trust in God**, then we will gain EVERYTHING. We will gain EVERYTHING simply because EVERYTHING comes from God, and He <u>withholds nothing good</u> from those who walk uprightly.

If we refuse **Trust in God** and hold on to trust in self, seeking things for ourselves, we may end up gaining everything the world has to offer, and be its friend.

But the world is deceptive. Deception: The mindset of the world tries to take all of God's good creation and put their own name on it, seeking to take credit for that <u>which it did not make</u>. But all that is gained, God will take away.

If we do so, we have exchanged our eternal treasures for eternal punishment. **I would much rather make reservations for eternity in Paradise, than for eternity in the Lake of Fire.**

"For whoever has,

to him shall be given,

and he shall have more abundance:

but whoever does not have, from him

shall be taken away even that which he

has... For to everyone that has shall be

given, and he shall have abundance:

but from him that does not have shall

be taken away even that which he has."

Matthew 13:12, 25:29

Concerning love, the greatest of all human needs: God always comes first, love follows.

"God is love."
1 John 4:8

God always comes first, so **Trust in God** comes first. We need not make an effort towards having love in our hearts, because it comes out of **Trust in God**. Love is birthed from **Trust in God** but it is not the love the world runs after.

No effort can be made to love, because God is a person and moves by His presence. Where the presence of God is, there is love. Where the presence of God is not, there is no love.

We see Jesus' in John's vision, the man he gave in adoption to his mother, to replace his relationship with her at his death. It is a good place to go if we are feeling loveless.

"The Revelation of Jesus Christ ...Jesus Christ, <u>who</u> is the faithful witness, <u>and</u> the first begotten of the dead, and the prince of the kings of the earth. To him that loved us, and  washed us from our sins in his own blood, and has made us kings and priests to God and his Father; to him <u>be</u> glory and dominion forever and ever. Amen. See, he comes with clouds; and every eye shall see him, and they <u>also</u> which pierced him: and all kindreds of the earth shall wail because of him. Even so, Amen. I am Alpha and Omega, the beginning and the ending, says the Lord, which is, and which was, and which is to come, the Almighty...I am Alpha and Omega, the first and the last: ... I saw seven golden candlesticks; and in the middle of the seven candlesticks <u>one</u> like to the Son of man, clothed with a garment down to the foot, and fastened about the waist with a golden girdle. His head and <u>his</u> hairs <u>were</u> white like wool, as white as snow; and his eyes <u>were</u> as a flame of fire; and his feet like fine brass, as if they burned in a furnace; and his voice as the sound of many waters. And he had in his right hand seven stars: and out of his mouth went a sharp two edged sword: and his countenance <u>was</u> as the sun shines in his strength. And when I saw him, I fell at his feet as dead. And he laid his right hand upon me, saying to me, Fear not; <u>I am</u> the first and the last: I am he that lives, and was dead; and, see, I am alive forevermore, Amen; and I have the keys of hell and of death." Revelation 1

God calls Himself the Alpha and the Omega, the beginning and the ending, the first and the last. We should always be excited to run to Him! He is the source of all life! As I recently stated, "Where the presence of God is, there is love," and, "Where the presence of God is not, there is no love." There may perhaps be lust imitating love, but not love.

Jesus said, "**<u>Scripture cannot be broken</u>**." It says,

> *"The end of the commandment is love out of a pure heart, and of a good conscience and of genuine faith."*
> *1 Timothy 1:5*

Thus, the imitation of love, lust, becomes the greatest enemy of mankind. Lust veiled as love is most deadly, and it is the <u>ultimate poison and gravest danger</u> to all.

GOD'S ESTIMATION OF WOMEN OF SEDUCTION:
Scripture by King Solomon, the son of King David:

"Her house is the way to **hell**, going down to the chambers of **death**." "For her house inclines to **death**, and her paths to the **dead**. None that go to her return again, neither do they take hold of the paths of life." (Proverbs 7: 27, 2:19). "To keep thee from the evil woman, from the flattery of the tongue of a strange woman. Lust not after her beauty in your heart neither let her take you with her eyelids. For by means of a whorish woman A man is brought to a piece of bread: and the adulteress **will hunt for the precious life**." ..."the **dead** are there;... her guests are in the depths of **hell**." (Proverbs 6: 25, 26 9:18).

New Testament Scriptures say that this is one of the few things to **RUN AWAY** from ! ! ! ! ! ! ! "Run away from fornication. Every sin that a man does is without the body; but he that commits fornication sins against his own body." (I Corinthians 6:18). "Run away from youthful lusts:" (II Tim 2: 22).

Lust is the **ultimate deception** of true love and truth. It is also the **ultimate transgression** against freedom. This is because it magnetizes and draws people, not allowing for a free-will choice but instead controlling by seduction. God, on the other hand, releases us from all lust through the element of **Trust in God**, and in so doing gives us true freedom. The reason is, that in **Trust in God** there is no magnetizing or seduction, but perfect freedom for us in which to **exercise** our free-will choice, without being manipulated, controlled, or under the influence of another person or power.

Other enemies of **Trust in God** include: **ANYTHING** that takes our focus off of God. The source of the distraction doesn't matter, neither the kind, neither the amount, neither the power. **ANYTHING** that takes our minds off a simple meditation of God, works against our **Trust in God**. When we are free from distractions, then we can **Trust in God**, remembering Him, seeing Him, experiencing His glories in us, around us, and through us, and observing Jesus in our behaviors that match His character.

Trust in God makes people entirely independent and self-sufficient. This is simply because it is a <u>personal choice</u> to have total reliance on God. God is totally self-sufficient and needs no one to provide for Him. God needs no one to <u>help Him to be God</u>, or to make Him who He is. **However, in God's church, families, communities, and the family of humanity, God enjoys our interdependency in the natural realm. It is God taking care of His own body.** "We then that are strong ought to bear the infirmities of the weak, and not to please ourselves. Let every one of us please his neighbor for his good to edification. For even Christ pleased not himself..." (Romans 15:1-3).

"Bear one another's burdens and so fulfill the law of Christ."

Galatians 6:2

"Now therefore perform the doing of it; that as there was a readiness to will, so there may be a performance . . . . For if there be first a willing mind, it is accepted according to what a man has, and not according to what he does not have. For I do not mean that other men be eased, and you burdened: But by an equality, that now at this time your abundance may be a supply for their want, that their abundance also may be a supply for your want: that there may be equality:

2 Corinthians 8:11-14

Personal Notes, Thoughts

In Christ we are all one. When a person is in total reliance on God he gives God all glory for meeting his needs and necessities. God will support and honor him and glorify Himself in him. God will also teach him to be a giver of good things to others.

Apostle Paul said through the inspiration of the Holy Spirit:

"I have learned, in whatever state I am in, to be content… everywhere and in all things I am instructed both to be full and to be hungry, both to abound and to suffer need. I can do all things through Christ who strengthens me…But my God shall supply all your need according to his riches in glory by Christ Jesus. Now to God and our Father be glory forever and ever. Amen." (Philippians 4: 11-13, 19-20).

So the ultimate way of life *is simple, very simple, so simple*, that **EVERYONE** misses it, except for only a few. That is why Jesus said,

"Enter in at the straight gate, for wide is the gate, and broad is the way, that leads to destruction, and many there be which go in at that place: because straight is the gate, and narrow is the way, which leads to life, and few there be that find it."

Matthew 7:13,14

A person may think that **Trust in God** would de-energize people, but just the opposite is true. If a person gains the mental state of resting in God it releases a surge of energy that comes from God Himself. Who could be more energized than God? There is no one like God who never runs out of energy. He is the true energizing bunny, so to speak, that continues on forever. And those that know God <u>will</u> live forever, with <u>more</u> energy than the energizing bunny, continually and forever !!! Amazing !!! God will make our hearts beat faithfully forever. Will we have blood in our resurrected bodies? When Jesus was risen from the dead and His disciples were scared of Him because they thought He was a spirit, He said, "**Touch me and feel me, a spirit does not have flesh and bones as you see that I have.**" He made no mention of blood. **What will we be made of?** But that is not the subject of this book! On the other hand, to ponder such things does help to instill a…

Childlike Trust.

From a state of Trust in God, a perfect rest in, and intimacy with God, God gives ideas, inspirations, new thoughts, and dreams we hadn't imagined before. He opens up to us new avenues of expression, expanding our horizons of view. This brings God Himself into our world, His world, without effort, human effort. This will happen with the joy of God. Nehemiah spoke to God's people about joy. (Nehemiah 8:10),

> *"This day is holy to the LORD your God; mourn not, nor weep . . . for the joy of the LORD is your strength."*

We will be enjoying life, resting in God without hindrances, confusion in complexities of human relationships, misunderstandings, and disappointments, for all comes from God, and God is all, and in all. As the Apostle Paul wrote in the holy Scripture, *"...Christ is all, and in all."* (Colossians 3:11).

The king shall joy in your strength, O LORD; and in your salvation how greatly shall he rejoice! You have given him his heart's desire, and have not withheld the request of his lips. Selah. For you satisfy him with the blessings of goodness: you set a crown of pure gold on his head. He asked life of you, <u>and</u> you gave <u>it</u> to him, <u>even</u> length of days forever and ever. His glory <u>is</u> great in your salvation: honor and majesty you have laid upon him. For you have made him most blessed forever: you have made him exceedingly glad with your countenance.

"For the king trusts in the *LORD*, and through the mercy of the most High he shall not be moved. Your hand shall find out all your enemies: your right hand shall find out those that hate you. You shall make them as a fiery oven in the time of your anger: the *LORD* shall swallow them up in his wrath, and the fire shall devour them... Be exalted, *LORD*, in your own strength: <u>so</u> we will sing and praise your power."

Psalms 21:1-9, 13

Paul the Apostle, who called himself a "bond slave of Jesus Christ," wrote:

"...our dear fellow servant, who is for you a faithful minister of Christ; who also **declared to us your love in the Spirit. For this cause we also, since the day we heard <u>it</u>**, do not stop praying for you, and to desire that you might be filled with the knowledge of his will in all wisdom and spiritual understanding; that you might walk worthy of the Lord unto all pleasing, being fruitful in every good work and increasing in the knowledge of God; strengthened with all might, according to his glorious power, unto all patience and longsuffering with joyfulness; Giving thanks to the Father, who has made us acceptable to be partakers of the inheritance of the saints in light: Who has delivered us from the power of darkness, and has translated <u>us</u> into the kingdom of his dear Son: In whom we have redemption through his blood, <u>even</u> the forgiveness of sins: who is the image of the invisible God, the firstborn of every creature: For by him were all things created, that are in heaven,

and that are in earth, visible and invisible, whether <u>they be</u> thrones, or dominions, or principalities, or powers; all things were created by him, and for him: And he is before all things, and by him all things consist. And he is the head of the body, the church; who is the beginning, the firstborn from the dead; that in all <u>things</u> he might have the preeminence. For it pleased <u>the Father</u> that in him should all fullness dwell; And having made peace through the blood of his cross, by him to reconcile all things to himself; by him, I <u>say</u>, whether <u>they be</u> things in earth, or things in heaven. And you, that were sometimes alienated and enemies in <u>your</u> mind by wicked works, yet now he has reconciled in the body of his flesh through death, to present you holy and unblameable and unreproveable in his sight; If you continue in the faith grounded and settled, and be not moved away from the hope of the gospel, which you have heard, and which was preached to every creature which is under heaven; of which I Paul am made a minister: " (Colossians 1: 7-23).

Paul the Apostle continues:

"*Even the mystery
which has been hidden
from ages
and from generations,
but now is made manifest
to his saints:
to whom God would make known
what is the riches of the glory
of this mystery
among the Gentiles; which is
Christ in you,
the hope of glory:*"

Colossians 1: 26,27

Personal Notes, Thoughts

"See that you refuse not him that speaks."

For if they did not escape who refused him that spoke on earth, much more we <u>shall not</u> escape, if we turn away from him that <u>speaks</u> from heaven:

Whose voice then shook the earth: but now he has promised, saying, Yet once more I shake not the earth only, but also heaven. And this word, Yet once more, signifies the removing of those things that are shaken, as of things that are made, that those things which cannot be shaken may remain. So since we are receiving a kingdom which cannot be moved,

let us have grace,
by which we may serve God acceptably with reverence and godly fear:

"For our God is a consuming fire."
(Hebrews 12:25-29).

Integration of Prayer into Trust in God

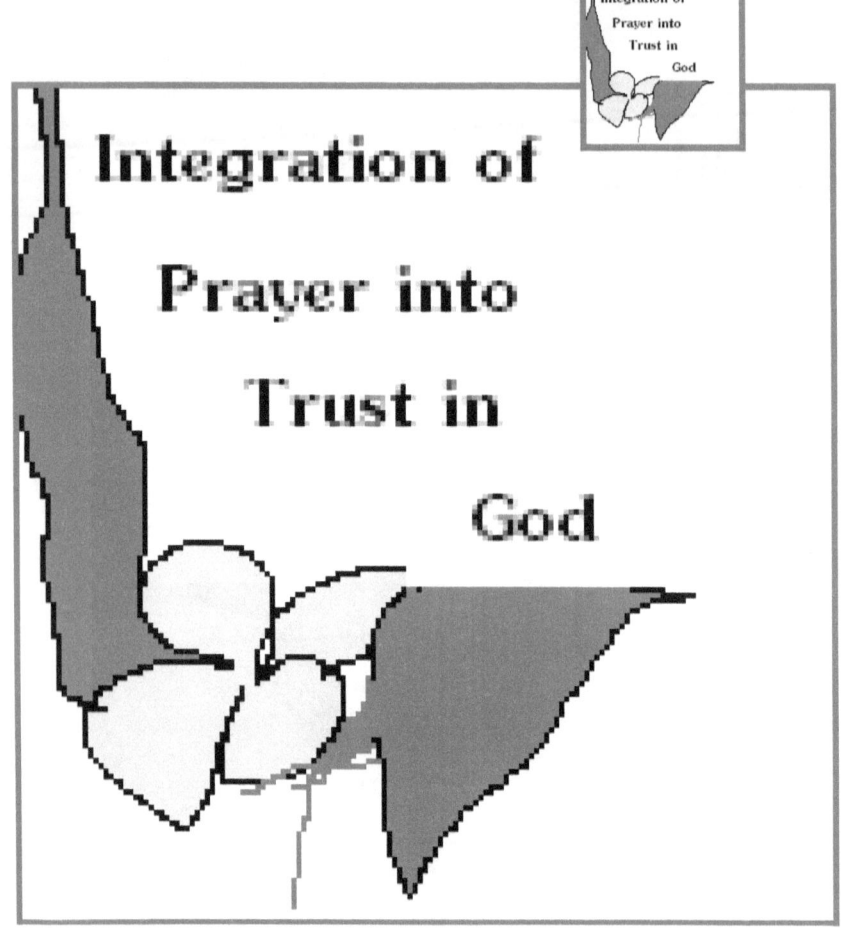

Integration or Prayer into Trust in God, Ponderings

God is right here with us and seeks communication with us whether it is silent or noisy. We are given instruction to be, **"Praying always with all prayer and supplication in the Spirit, and watching to that end with all perseverance and supplication for all saints."** (Ephesians 6:18).

I sense God's compassion when I wait quietly on Him and in this way learn to **Trust in God** more. Also, as I see people helped by the prayers of others and their dedication to help others in many tangible ways, I also learn to **Trust in God** more. I sense our compassionate God at work in me when I wait quietly on Him in prayer, and I like to observe and witness His compassionate work in me and in those around me.

Jesus spoke with confidence concerning prayer saying:

"Have faith in God. For truly I say to you, That whoever shall say to this mountain, Be removed, and be thrown into the sea; and shall not doubt in his heart, but shall believe that those things which he says shall come to pass; he shall have whatever he says. Therefore I say to you, Whatever things you desire, when you pray, believe that you receive <u>them</u>, and you shall have <u>them</u>. And when you stand praying, forgive"

Mark 11:22-25

Jesus said, "**From the beginning of time the kingdom of heaven suffers violence and the violent take it by force.**" As we get to know God and *Trust in God* we learn to be like Him, to be bold and courageous in our faith, as God is in His. Boldness and courage are part of the rainbow of God's character traits. As they develop in us we will enjoy seeing these attributes of God at work in us, and **"WHEN YOU (WE) STAND PRAYING (WE) FORGIVE."** and God will be pleased and move through us. Jesus said,

> Truly, truly, I say to you, "whatever you shall ask the Father in my name, he will give it to you. So far you have asked nothing in my name: ask, and you shall receive, that your joy may be full."
>
> John 16: 23-24

"And this is the confidence that we have in him, that, if we ask anything according to his will, he hears us: And if we know that he hears us, whatever we ask, we know that we have the petitions that we desired of him." (1 John 5: 14, 15).

I like to think of it this way: as a blank check, a "fill-in-the-blank" in a student's workbook, or a "fill-in-the-blank" on one of my <u>Pastor Wolfson's handouts for taking sermon notes</u>. Once the blank is filled in, it becomes part of the document, part of the text. Once the blank check is written out, it becomes that amount. It was <u>God</u>, not I, that put in that promise, a "fill-in-the-blank" into His very own Scriptures saying basically, "Fill-in-the-blank" _____ with whatever you desire !!! <u>It was not</u> I that gave that offer, <u>God</u> did. So whatever I choose to put in the blank becomes a part of God's own textbook, His own Holy Scripture!

Amazing !!!!!!!

After I ask God for something, I like to read His own Word back to Him, complete with my answer to His own "fill-in-the-blank" question. I like to do this with total and complete confidence. <u>God</u> said it, I didn't! So I may say back, "The Word of God says_____, and put in the exact same things for which I asked God. I believe that if I say it out loud, I am following the instructions Jesus gave us, and **<u>if and when I ever believe it in my heart, it shall happen as Jesus said</u>**!

My problem is, all the good Word of God has to get past my outer self and deep into my core. But that takes: – **PERSISTENCE – FORBEARANCE – DETERMINATION – COMMITMENT – ENDURANCE – STICK-TO-TIVENESS** – and I am not usually willing or prepared to put this forth. Because of that, I leave myself incapable of handling God's promises properly and effectively. Gradually we grow in **Trust in God**, and in **Knowledge of God**. We increase our learning and experience in these areas through **exercise**. We gradually get stronger.

We increase in bold, courageous faith, as **Knowledge of God** grows upon **Knowledge of God** in us, and our **Trust in God** grows upon our **Trust in God**. Growing in this aspect, is part of maturing and growing up in Jesus, getting to know our persistent, committed, and faithful God. Our Heavenly Father gives us the supreme example of

persistence.

Jesus taught us to pray directly to our Heavenly Father in His, Jesus' name. As we seek God's face we must always pray and make requests in Jesus' name. Those are Jesus' instructions. It is an exercise of childlike trust to follow Jesus' instructions, and learn to ask God for help to do His will, develop our talents, fulfill our dreams, and enjoy Him in every aspect of our lives as we live in this beautiful world He created for us. We are taught to get to know God in a humble way, as little children. **Jesus also taught us that agreement in prayer is**

POWERFUL:

"Truly I say to you,
whatever you shall
bind on earth shall be bound
in heaven: and whatever you shall
loose on earth shall be loosed in heaven.
Again I say to you, that if
two of you
shall agree on earth as touching anything
that they shall ask,
it shall be done for them of my Father
which is in heaven.
For where two or three are
gathered together in my name,
there I am in the midst of them."
Matthew 18:18-20

Personal Notes, Thoughts

Jesus encourages us to have confidence in our Heavenly Father and in His willingness to give to us every good and perfect gift as we agree with each other, come to oneness of heart and mind, get along peacefully with one another, come to settled decisions, and share visions; and as we hope, expect and anticipate together new horizons and realms of thought. God emphasizes agreement and peace and wants us to work together hand in hand, as we trust God's judgements. When we wait on God in prayer, we are waiting for the Holy Spirit, like wind, not knowing exactly when He will come or how. This teaches us to trust in God's judgements concerning every situation and in His decision making power. God decides how and when His Spirit moves. Jesus said,

> "The wind blows wherever it goes,
> and you hear the sound of it but can
> not tell where it came from, and
> where it going:
> so also is every one that is
> born of the Spirit."

Our **Trust in God**, and dependence on Him is further magnified through the **Baptism of the Holy Spirit**. We first hear of the **Baptism of the Holy Spirit** in John 1: 29-34. When John the Baptist saw Jesus for the first time he shouted,

Behold,
the Lamb of God
which takes away
the sin of the world . . .

This is he of whom I said, After me comes a man who is before me, for he was before me. And I didn't know him: but for the purpose that he would be made manifest to Israel, that is why I have come baptizing with water. And John bare record, saying, I saw the Spirit descending from heaven like a dove, and it remained on him. And I didn't know him: but he that sent me to baptize with water, the same said to me,

Upon whom you shall see the Spirit descending, and remaining on him, the same is he who baptizes with the Holy Spirit. And I saw, and bare record that this is the Son of God."

This is the first historical account of the announcement of the ministry of Jesus Christ, God's Only Begotten Son, and within it, we see God refers to the **Baptism of the Holy Spirit**. God shows His high regard for the **Baptism of the Holy Spirit**. Jesus <u>shouted</u> about the **Baptism of the Holy Spirit** on the last day of the feast, at the Jewish Feast of Tabernacles (John 7: 37): "In the last <u>day</u>, the great day of the feast, Jesus stood up and shouted,

*If any man thirst,
let him come to me,
and drink.
He that believes on me,
as the scripture has said,
out of his innermost being shall flow
rivers of living water.
(But this he spoke of the Spirit,
which they that believe on him
would receive;
for the Holy Spirit was
not yet given; because Jesus was
not yet glorified)."*

John 7:37-39

Jesus spoke clearly of it again, after he came alive from the dead. Before he rose up to be with his Father, he

ANNOUNCED

the coming **Baptism of the Holy Spirit**. Jesus said to his disciples:

"Wait for the promise of the Father,

which...you have heard about from me,
for John truly baptized with water, but you shall be

baptized with the Holy Spirit

not many days from now ... you shall receive power, after the Holy Spirit has come upon you: and you shall be witnesses to me both in Jerusalem, and in all Judea, and in Samaria, and to the uttermost part of the earth." Acts 1

Historical account: "...And when the day of Pentecost was fully come, they were all in one accord in one place. And suddenly there came a sound from heaven like a rushing mighty wind, and it filled the whole house where they were sitting. And there appeared to them like tongues of fire, and it sat on each of them. And they were all filled with the Holy Spirit, and began to speak with other tongues, as the Spirit gave them utterance... Now when this news noisily spread abroad, the multitudes came together, and were confounded, because every man heard them speak in his own language. And they were all amazed and marveled..." (Acts 2:2-7).

Through the **Baptism of the Holy Spirit** our dependency on Christ can be clearly seen. We also have the great privilege and honor to find out more about the power of prayer in order to more substantially help God's children. We need to try to fulfill God's work in the earth as He instructed, and seek to rise to the heights to which we were created to attain. We can be brought closer to God's apex for us by including

The Father's great promise:

the Baptism of the Holy Spirit.

The Baptism of the Holy Spirit is gained simply by asking our Heavenly Father for it in Jesus' name. I have already quoted the following, but it is prominent as a foundational Scripture to help instill childlike Trust in God into our hearts, and so is worth repeating: Jesus said,

> *"If a son asks bread of any of you that is a father,*
>
> *will you give him a rock?*
>
> *Or if <u>he asks</u> for fish,*
>
> *will you give him a snake?*
>
> *Or if he asks for an egg,*
>
> *will you offer him a scorpion?*
>
> *If you then being evil,*
>
> *know how to give good gifts to your children:*
>
> *how much more shall <u>your</u> Heavenly Father*
>
> *give the Holy Spirit to them that ask him."*

Integration of Prayer into Trust in God

The Holy Spirit may come like a mighty rushing wind to a person waiting on God, or as a gentle quiet breeze, or without any feelings, as was in my case. I finally took God at His Word, by trust, instead of by evidence. Sometimes the **Baptism of the Holy Spirit** with speaking in "tongues" comes immediately when someone asks, other times after waiting on God, and still other times it comes simply as an act of faith on God's promise. Every one of us is different and God works in mysterious ways His wonders to perform.

In learning to **Trust in God** more, there is yet another avenue we can explore, the avenue of *persistence*, in other words, not giving up. God wants us to have the dreams and desires of our hearts fulfilled, that have come from Him, and were birthed in His heart first, and so in reality are God's dreams. But if we pursue our own selfish dreams we are just...

– wasting our time – wasting our life away – cause selfishness never please our Heavinly Daddy.

Apostle James warns about this in Scripture:

"Where do wars and fighting <u>come</u> from among you? Don't they <u>come, even come</u> from your lusts that war in your members? You lust, and do not have; you kill, and desire to have, and cannot obtain; you fight and war; yet you do not have, because you do not ask. You ask, and do not receive, because you ask amiss, that you may consume it on your lusts. You adulterers and adulteresses, don't you know that the friendship with the world is being an enemy of God? Whoever therefore will be a friend of the world is the enemy of God. Do you think that the scripture says in vain, 'The spirit that lives in us lusts to envy?' But he gives more grace. So he says, God resists the proud, but gives grace to the humble. Submit yourselves therefore to God. Resist the devil, and he will run from you. Draw near to God, and he will draw near to you. Cleanse <u>your</u> hands, <u>you</u> sinners; and purify <u>your</u> hearts, <u>you</u> double minded. Be afflicted, and mourn, and weep; let your laughter be turned to mourning, and <u>your</u> joy to heaviness. Humble yourselves in the sight of the Lord, and he shall lift you up. " (James 4:1-10).

*But God doesn't want us to get discouraged in
following after our dreams, that are His dreams.
He doesn't want us to give up or lose enthusiasm.
He wants us to continue to pursue,
like the woman in Jesus' parable (story).
She wouldn't give up knocking on someone's door
until they got so irritated they opened the door
and granted her request in order to stop the knocking.
She got everything for which she asked.*

Jesus taught us that God, in the same way, will open doors of opportunity and blessing, as we keep asking, seeking, and knocking. That is how he responds as we choose Him with our:

God given free-will choice.
Free-will choice is a great gift from God.
He will in no way step on our freedom.
It allows us to honor, or walk on, the blood of God.

He waits for us to knock on heaven's door. It is possible to find the LORD our God by using our free-will. We can freely choose Him! As Jesus said,

> *"Freely you have received, freely give."*
> *Matthew 10:8*

However, we can't have *Him* by obligation. *He* wants us to come to *Him* freely. We can't have *Him* by obligation, manipulation, seduction, domination, intimidation, or for reputation, but we can have *Him*. Anyone can have *Him*. They can have *Him* just by choosing *Him* with their free-will choice. It is the only way to have a relationship with God. *He* is a God of freedom. That is why we can enter into *His* presence by waiting on *Him* quietly in prayer. We can wait for *Him* to give us something to say to *Him* that comes out of a true, genuine choice of heart, not from pressure. Our relationship with God is <u>not built on obligation</u> but on free-will choice. After God chose Abraham, and he chose God, God said, Genesis 15:1, "Fear not, Abram: I <u>am</u> thy shield, <u>and</u> thy exceeding great reward."

We can ask, seek, and knock on heaven's door until we finally discover that He is our life. Once we make this discovery we can delve into life itself, and know that every ounce, every particle, every bit of life is an expression of God's beautiful person. And every opportunity is an opportunity to:

get to TRUST God more and more and more and more and more...

Then we keep pursuing and keep going. We learn to Trust in God more and more, not holding anything back from Him. And we begin to get a fuller knowledge of Him as we continually rest in Him. Our sense of **Trust in God** will grow forever as will our **Knowledge of God**!!! In teaching us to **Trust in God**, Jesus also mentioned about praying privately and in simplicity, saying,

But you, when you pray, enter into your private room, and when you have shut your door, pray to your Father which is in secret; and your Father who sees in secret shall reward you openly. But when you pray, Do not use vain repetitions, as the heathen <u>do</u>: for they think that they shall be heard for their much speaking. Therefore do not be like them: for your Father knows what things you have need of, before you ask him. Therefore pray in this way:

*Our Father
who art in heaven,
Hallowed be thy name.
Thy kingdom come. Thy will be
done in earth, as <u>it is</u> in heaven.
Give us this day our daily bread.
And forgive us our debts,
as we forgive our debtors.
And lead us not into temptation,
but deliver us from evil:
For thine is the kingdom,
and the power, and the glory, forever.
Amen."*

Matthew 6:6-13

Also, the element of truth, is an essential ingredient as we draw near to God. He calls Himself the "God of truth" (Isaiah 65:16). Without truth, we have nothing, we are nothing. Without truth there is no existence, just dust, or something that passes away like a long forgotten memory. But truth is eternal. Truth is God. God is truth. Jesus said,

> "I am the way, the truth, and the life."
> "Whoever hears the truth will listen to my voice."

If there is no truth, then there is nothing on which <u>even to begin</u> a relationship with God. So we wait in His presence. We wait and wait until we get real, until we are real before Him. Then He can really help us, and help us make the first steps in coming to Him, with some honest words from an earnest desire to really get to know Him. God is so good and so patient and so kind. He actually waits to hear our first sincere cry for Him, "And therefore will the LORD wait, that he may be gracious to you...he will be very gracious to you at the voice of your cry; when he shall hear it, he will answer you." (Isaiah 30:18).

*That he who blesses
himself in the earth
shall bless himself in the God of truth;
and he that swears
in the earth
shall swear by the God of truth;
because the former troubles
are forgotten, and because they are
hidden from my eyes.
For, see, I create new heavens
and a new earth:
and the former shall not be remembered,
nor come into mind."*

Isaiah 65:16,17

That is why it is good to wait quietly before God and seek to say something to Him that is real and genuine. Our Heavenly Father will not give heavenly rewards to those who pray to be seen and heard, to receive praise from man, and obtain the admiration of people. Jesus said those that do this, "...**have already received their reward.**" In other words, they have exchanged the praise and goodwill of their Heavenly Father, to get the praise and goodwill of people. This is like having many people in our heart and no room for the person of Jesus Christ, as I spoke about before, do we have

✡ **no room in the Inn of our heart for baby Jesus?** ✡

We need another ingredient for **Trust in God** to grow in our hearts. It is revelation! Ask God for revelation. **REVELATION = KNOWLEDGE REVEALED BY GOD** the Holy Spirit is constantly leading people into truth, those that want it, and so choose to listen to truth. Jesus said, **"When the Spirit of truth, is come, he will guide you into all truth: for he shall not speak of himself; but whatever he shall hear that shall he speak; and he will show you things to**

Integration of Prayer into Trust in God

come. He shall glorify me; for he shall receive of mine, and shall show it to you. All things that the Father has are mine; therefore I said, that he shall take of mine, and shall show it to you."** Our Heavenly Father is more than willing to grant revelation, but the Holy Spirit needs something to work with during the process of revelation. We are responsible to put something into our Father's hand. We put the Word of God into our Father's hand. Our God is a God of multiplication and growth, as He said to Noah after the flood, "While the earth remains, **seedtime and harvest**... shall not cease." (Genesis 8:22). We should always be planting good seeds into God's kingdom in our hearts and in others and expect a marvelous harvest from our

❦ *Farmer Father* ❦

Jesus taught us, **"Be careful what you hear: with what measure you measure out, it shall be measured to you; and to you that hear shall more be given."** Jesus also taught us:

Integration of Prayer into Trust in God

"The kingdom of heaven can be compared to a grain of mustard seed, which a man took, and sowed in his field: Which truly is the least of all seeds: but when it is grown, it is the greatest among herbs, and becomes a tree, so that the birds of the air come and live in the branches of it." (Matthew 13:31-32)

So it is with revelation. We put a Holy Scripture in our hearts, and that is what we put in our Heavenly Father's hand. The Holy Spirit will begin a discourse, an inner conversation with us. He will help us to ponder it in our minds, until we know what it means. It is a process, then a priceless treasure! For me, I like to think about a specific verse and try to figure out what it means. I seem to get a tiny bit of understanding a little at a time, not a lot. I get excited and stirred up to find out what it really means and to understand it more. Then I get it! This priceless treasure of revelation is greater than all the riches and treasures in all the world, and only comes from God, there is nowhere else to get it.

When understanding comes, it is deeply satisfying. It gives a deep and stable sense of security when I finally understanding "know that I know" what God meant. For me, there is nothing to be compared to it. It is truth, pure and clear! To know what my Heavenly Father really thinks about something is precious.

It is like finding the

which Jesus spoke of, worth more than anything, definitely greater than anything the world has to offer. As I hunger for more understanding concerning some Scripture, at times I feel in agony, like having a baby. Sometimes I have <u>extreme frustration</u> if I can't get what God meant. Other times I may have a feel for the truth, or understand some of it, but not have a <u>complete</u> understanding.

At those times I could say with Apostle Paul:

Integration of Prayer into Trust in God

"My little children, of whom I travail in birth again until Christ be formed in you." But in my case, *"I am in travail again until Christ be formed in me!"* But understanding seems to come gradually, like water seeping down into the soil to water a garden, or like the sun as it gradually arises and illumines the beautiful landscape, with all its intricacies, slowly increasing the colors and brilliant shades in God's creation around us.

In learning to **Trust in God**, God also encourages us to be continual in our prayer, our meditation and thoughts of Him, communion with Him and earnest requests to Him. God is right here with us, listening for our voice and our communication with Him, whether we think so or not. He waits for our voice.

However, if anyone is choosing from their heart, with their God given gift of freedom, to willingly walk in evil pathways, God will not hear their prayers, unless they're struggling within, and don't know how to overcome sin, darkness or evil.

Integration of Prayer into Trust in God

He speaks to His rebellious children through Isaiah,1:15-20. **"And when you spread forth your hands, I will hide my eyes from you: yes, when you make many prayers, I will not hear: your hands are full of blood. Wash yourselves, make yourselves clean; put away the evil of your doings from before my eyes; stop doing evil; learn to do well; seek judgment, relieve the oppressed, judge the fatherless, plead for the widow. Come now, and let us reason together, says the LORD: though your sins be as scarlet, they shall be as white as snow; though they be red like crimson, they shall be as wool. If you be willing and obedient, you shall eat the good of the land: But if you refuse and rebel, you shall be devoured with the sword: for the mouth of the LORD has spoken it."**

And to His people who have been in great sin, and suffered deep consequences, "And therefore will the LORD wait, that he may be gracious to you, and therefore he will be exalted, that he may have mercy on you... blessed are all they that wait for him... **you shall weep no more**:" (Isaiah 30:18, 19).

"You shall weep no more."

Suffering under our Heavenly Father's chastisement and then returning to Him to receive His mercy, develops a deep childlike **Trust in God**. We can read about this at great length in the book of Hebrews: "... seeing we also are encompassed about with so great a cloud of witnesses, let us lay aside every weight, and the sin which does so easily trap us, and let us run with patience the race that is set before us, looking to Jesus the author and finisher of our faith; who for the joy that was set before him endured the cross, despising the shame, and is set down at the right hand of the throne of God. For consider him that endured such contradiction of sinners against himself, lest you be wearied and faint in your minds. You have not yet resisted to blood, striving against sin. And you have forgotten the exhortation which speaks to you as to children, My son, despise not the chastening of the Lord, or faint when you are rebuked of him:

For whom the Lord loves he chastens, and scourges every son whom he receives. If you endure chastening, God deals with you as with sons; for what son is he whom the father does not chasten? But if you be without chastisement, of which all are partakers, then you are not born of the Father, and not sons. Furthermore we have had our natural fathers which corrected us, and we gave them reverence; shouldn't we much rather be in subjection to the Father of spirits, and live? For they truly for a few days chastened us after their own pleasure; but he for our profit, that we may be partakers of his holiness. Now no chastening for the present seems to be joyous, but grievous: nevertheless afterwards it yields the peaceful fruit of righteousness to them which are **exercised** by it." (Hebrews 12:1-11).

Conclusion

Conclusion to Trust in God, Ponderings

I discovered through God's revelation to me about **Trust in God**, that God was available to me in a very real way, that nothing had to hinder my faith in Him, and that <u>even I</u>, could live in a state of perfect **Trust in God**. This thrilled me when I discovered it, because I then knew God accepted me. Through reading the Scriptures, I know God always counts my faith as righteousness, and I <u>know</u> it perfectly pleases Him. **Trust in God** opened up the door for me to have a living faith in God and know His presence continually. I am <u>relieved from the fear</u> of going to the Eternal Lake of Fire, and have the joy of knowing that I am always pleasing to God when I am trusting Him. This gives me such joy and satisfaction. It perhaps is unimaginable to a person that has not experienced the years of uncertainty that I experienced, and then to be released into a peaceful rest in God that never ends or diminishes. It is like a river of peace deeper and wider than the Mississippi, truly

<u>Heaven on earth.</u>

Every second is eternal life for me when I trust in Him. As Jesus prayed, "Eternal life is to know you, the only true God, and Jesus Christ whom you have sent." It has given me such peace to the extent that I wish everyone could discover it, and to the extent that I wish there was something I could do to help someone else discover it, even for me to go to Hell and the Lake of Fire forever. Song-prayer: I began singing this, and teaching myself, "Know Jesus. Trust in Him." while He was setting me free !!

♫ *Getting to know You; getting to know all about You;* ♫

♫ *Learning to trust You; Getting to know that You care;* ♫

♫ *Asking that I will; Never leave You or forsake You;* ♫

♫ *Your blessings flow within and around me;* ♫

♫ *Showing me and helping me to see that;* ♫

♫ *You love me.* ♫

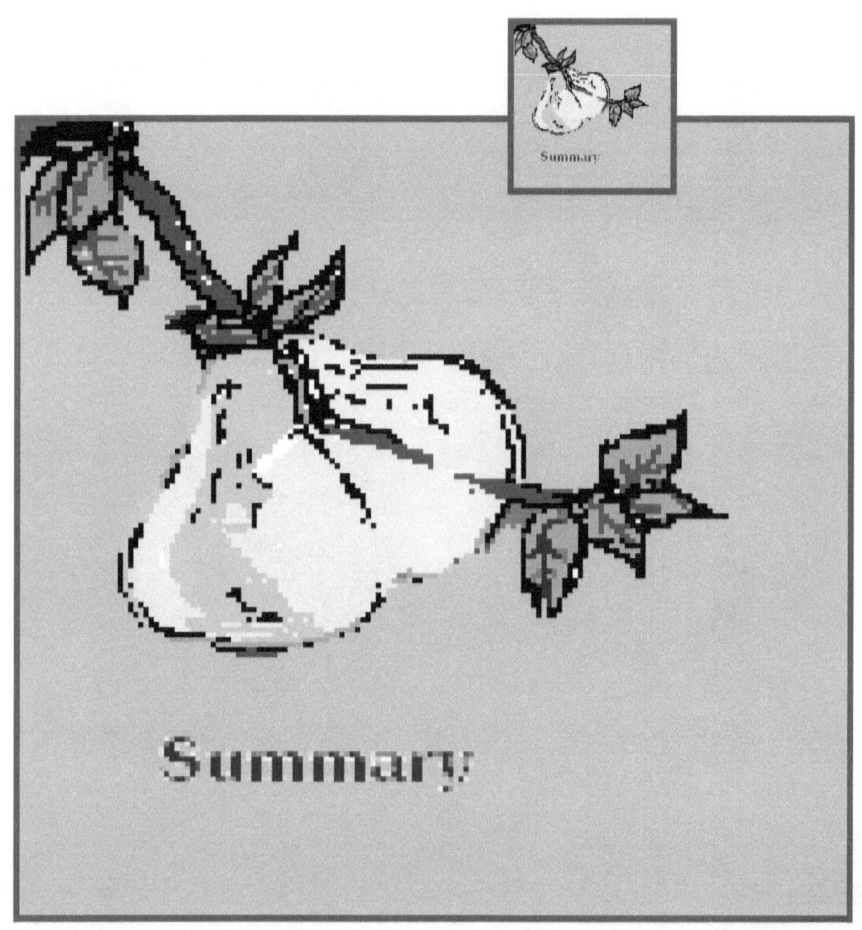

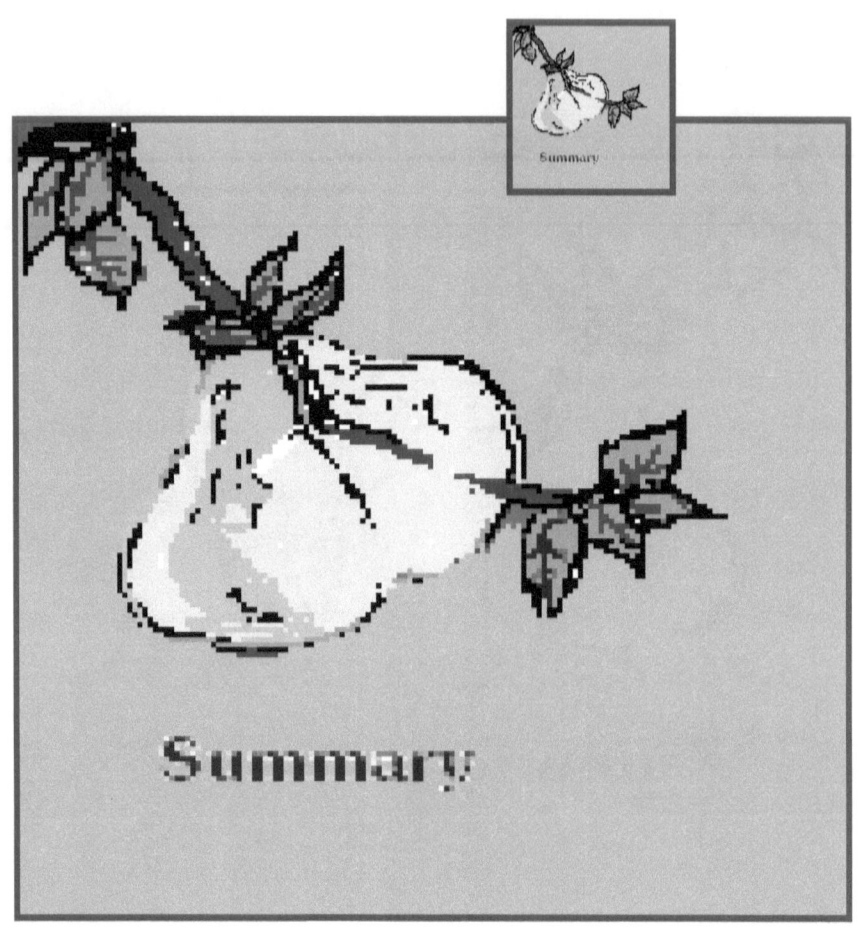

Summary to Trust in God, Ponderings

As we walk through life we have to decide where we will put our minds. Will they be on God, or on man, or on the various whirlwinds that come and go through our lives? God is not a whirlwind, always changing & unpredictable, without a foundation. The Bible teaches that God is

changeless:

"Jesus Christ

the same yesterday,
and today, and forever."
Hebrew 13:8

the Father of lights,
with whom there is no variableness,
neither shadow of turning."
James 1:17

If we put our **Trust in God** we can be sure that it's a **STRONG FOUNDATION**, one that will never change and one that will never go away, and He will not change His mind. God is sure and stable, forever and forever. That is **TRUE STABILITY**. That is **ETERNAL LIFE**. That is **ETERNAL SECURITY**. That is **STRENGTH, POWER, ASSURANCE,** and also includes incredible **WONDER, PURITY,** and **HOLINESS** and **EVERYTHING** which comes along with God, which is **EVERYTHING**.

> *For whoever has,*
> *to him shall be given,*
> *and he shall have more abundance."*
> *Matthew 13:12*

because God's blessings keep coming forever, without any stop to them, or His holding back. They just keep coming, and coming and coming. And He never will decide to stop blessing us, because He is God. That is His nature and He is eternal love.

He just keeps giving... and giving... and giving...

That is His divine nature, and that is the divine nature that He has put in us, His own nature. 2 Peter 1: 4 states:

> "Whereby are given to us
> exceeding
> great and precious promises:
> that by these you may be partakers
> of the
> divine nature,
> having escaped the corruption
> that is in the world
> through lust."

So **Trust in God** is heaven, it is life forevermore, it is eternal life in the here and now. **Trust in God** brings His life to us, in us, and through us. It is exceptional. There is nothing like it. There is nothing but it. There is nothing but God.

Summary

But, there must be a marriage. **Trust in God** must be married to **Knowledge of God**, or else we will end up with a marital partner other than God. We will find ourselves with a lie, with darkness, with nothing at all. So then we must be open to what God has **really** revealed Himself to be, <u>even if we don't like it</u>, and what He **really** is made of, and what His emotions really are, and what His feelings really are about various issues. That is, if we **really** want to get to know Him, and belong to God. We will say from deep within our hearts, "Give me the real God. I will trust Him as He is. I will trust Him exactly as He has revealed Himself, <u>and</u> reveals Himself to be. If I trust Him, I know that He will take care of me, and I don't have to be afraid of His judgements, because He will use His mighty power to protect and defend me, and destroy those that would destroy me." Then we can rest. Our **Trust in God** grows. Our **Knowledge of God** grows. We are without fear forever. We are with Him forever and in His arms forever. <u>So let the marriage begin</u>, if it has not been, and let it <u>remain the same</u> and never be changed for another. For God alone is our life.

Forever and ever. So be it!!!

"And we know
that we are of God,
and the whole world lies in wickedness.
And we know
that the Son of God is come,
and has given us an understanding,
that we may know him
that is true,
and we are in him
that is true,
even in his Son Jesus Christ.
this is the true God, and eternal life.
Little children, keep yourselves
from idols. Amen.
1 John 5:21

"In the beginning God created the heaven and the earth."
Bible, Old Testament, Genesis 1:1

"And I saw a new heaven and a new earth: for the first heaven and the first earth were passed away;..."
Bible, New Testament, Revelation 21:1

The Marriage

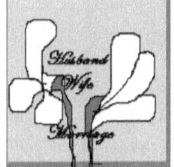

Knowledge of God

to

Trust in God

"We know that whoever is born of God does not sin; but he that is born of God keeps himself, and that wicked one does not touch him. <u>And</u> we know that we are of God, and the whole world lies in wickedness. And we know that the Son of God is come, and has given us an understanding, that we may know him that is true, and we are in him that is true, <u>even</u> in his Son Jesus Christ. This is the true God, and eternal life. Little children, keep yourselves from idols. Amen."
Bible, New Testament, 1 John 5:18-21

"Christ also loved the church, and gave himself for it

that he might sanctify and cleanse it

with the washing of water by the word

that he might present it to himself a glorious church,

not having spot, or wrinkle,

or any such thing;

but that it should be holy and without blemish.

So ought men to love their wives as their own bodies.

He that loves his wife loves himself.

For no man ever yet hated his own flesh; but nourishes and

cherishes it,

even as the Lord the church:

For we are members of his body, of his flesh, and of his bones.

For this cause shall a man leave his father and mother,

and shall be joined to his wife,

and they two shall be one flesh.

This is a great mystery:

but I speak concerning Christ and the church."

(Ephesians 5:25-32)

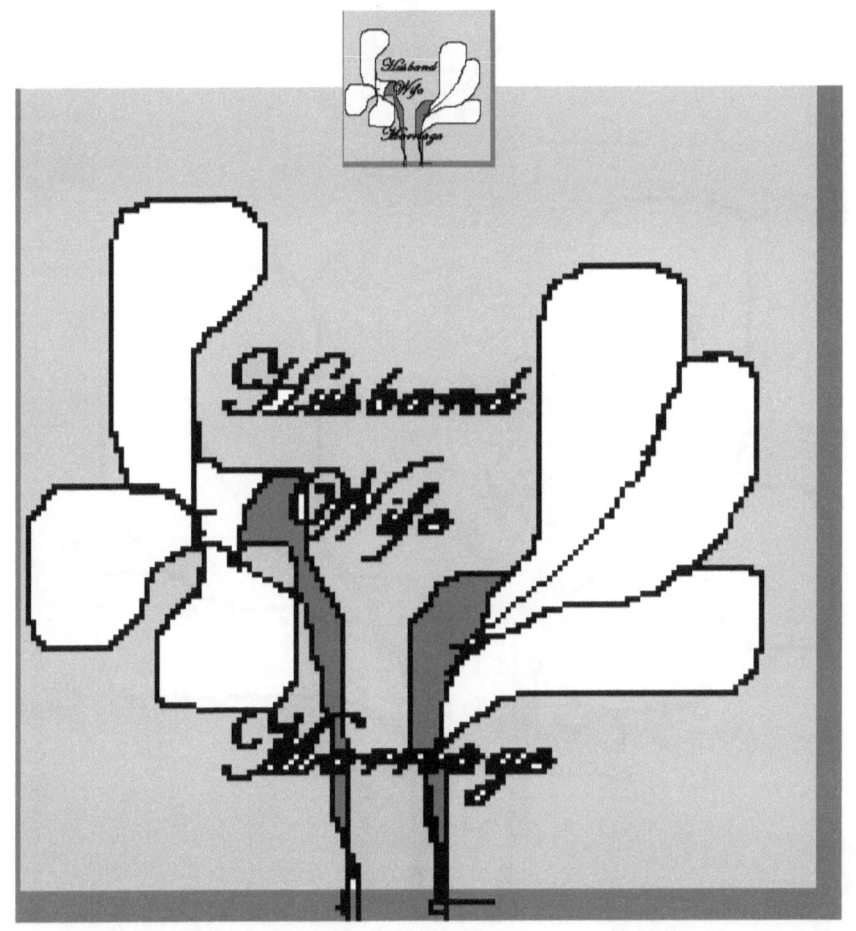

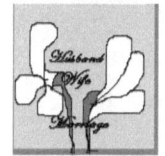

Marriage of Knowledge of God to Trust in God

I live, breath, walk, talk, eat, and live only for this:

The Marriage of: Knowledge of God to Trust in God

In any marriage there is a relationship. The marriage occurs because of the depths of the relationship. To enter into depths with God, we must establish a relationship with Him. For our relationship with God to be as substantial as an earthly marriage, we must have a **POINT OF CONTACT.** This **POINT OF CONTACT** may be different for everyone. It is whatever makes God real to us personally. Scripture teaches in Isaiah, "...the lambs shall feed after their manner," (5:17) they "shall lie down , and none shall make them afraid." (17: 2).

The lambs shall feed after <u>their</u> manner.

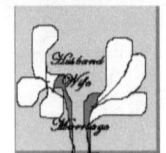

To enter into more depths of relationship with God we must:

FIRST: Care about making contact with God.

SECOND: Put away any idea that we're trying to impress God or earn His friendship, companionship or comradeship. Earning something is just having an employer. Impressing someone is just putting on an outward appearance, an outward covering. Neither of these forms a relationship. A relationship is an inward talking of the heart, not anything surface or superficial formed to impress or earn approval.

THIRD: Find a **POINT OF CONTACT** with God. A relationship is to delight in God, and delight in God in one another. And if it is truly relationship with God that we seek, then we take delight in Him. God says in Isaiah 58:14:

"Then you shall delight yourself in the LORD and I will cause you to ride upon the high places of the earth, and feed you with the heritage of Jacob, your father; for the mouth of the LORD has spoken it."

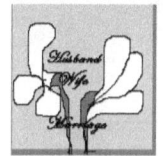

Through the Holy Spirit's revelations to John, Jesus' friend, we have learned from God about relationship and love:

> *"Beloved, let us love one another: for love is of God; and every one that loves is born of God, and knows God. He that does not love does not know God; for God is love. In this was manifested the love of God toward us, because that God sent his only begotten Son into the world, that we might live through him. Herein is love, not that we loved God, but that he loved us, and sent his Son to be the propitiation for our sins. Beloved, if God so loved us, we ought also to love one another. No man has seen God at any time. If we love one another, God lives in us, and his love is perfected in us."*
>
> *I John 4:7-12*

If we focus on **Trust in God** while we delight ourselves in **Knowledge of God**, we *escape* from self. God says in Isaiah: "...it shall come, that I will gather all nations and tongues; and they shall come, and see **my glory**; And I will set a sign

among them, and I will send those that *escape* of them to the nations...that have not heard my fame, neither have seen my glory, and they shall declare my glory among the Gentiles. And they shall bring all your brethren for an offering to the LORD out of all nations...to my holy mountain Jerusalem, says the LORD,..." (66:18-20). That is why **Trust in God** is essential. We are gluing our eyes on God, and letting Him be our EVERYTHING . He comes in, in waves of understanding, comprehension, inspiration, comfort, and compassion. He touches our innermost spiritual being, opens up our eyes to see Him, to be <u>able</u> to see Him in His Word, or in the wonders of His creation at which we are gazing. This becomes our **POINT OF CONTACT**. He unfolds us in His presence and expounds to us

Knowledge of God.

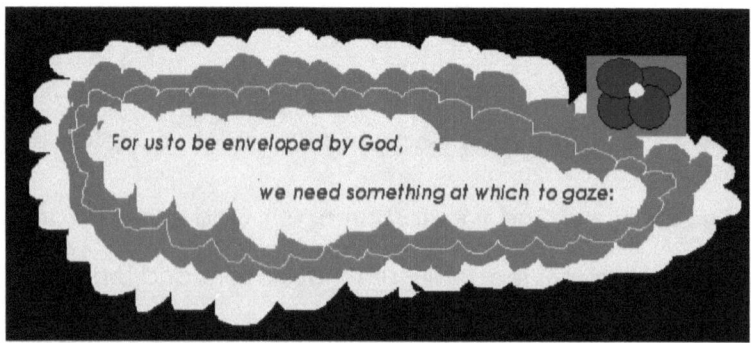

For us to be enveloped by God, we need something at which to gaze:

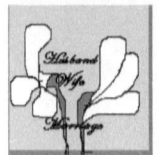

The Holy Spirit teaches us, but needs time to reach us.

He <u>needs time</u> to be able to reach us through all our complexities of thought, emotions, preconceptions, hurts, wounds, and personalities. "I will praise you; for I am fearfully <u>and</u> wonderfully made: marvelous <u>are</u> thy works; and <u>that</u> my soul knows right well." (Psalms 139:14). He opens our hearts. He softens our hearts. He helps us to relax in Him. He helps us enjoy His world around us.

As we think about something in God's good creation, and gaze on it, is identical to thinking about a word in God's Word. His person is <u>in</u> that word. His person <u>is</u> that word. His person <u>is</u> the message that God's good creation is speaking of His glory. It <u>is</u> that Word which has gone out into all the earth, and there is no language where it is not spoken. In God's good creation we can find a **POINT OF CONTACT** with

Almighty God.

"The heavens declare the glory of God;
and the firmament shows his handiwork.
Day to day utters speech,
and night to night shows knowledge.
There is no speech nor language,
where their voice is not heard.
Their line is gone out through all the earth,
and their words to the end of the world. . . ."

Psalm 19:1-4

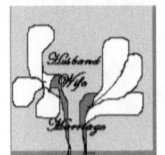

Also the Word of God which we read, is heralded by John, Jesus' close friend, in his gospel, the book of John, the fourth book of the New Testament, <u>first chapter, first verse</u>:

> *"In the beginning was the Word,
> and the Word was with God,
> and the Word was God."*
> *John 1:1*

But we do <u>need time</u> to eat and digest the Word of God our spiritual food, and grow in our Lord Jesus Christ. We <u>need time</u> to allow the Holy Spirit to reach and teach us. I guess that is why the five foolish virgins didn't make it into the wedding, in Jesus' story (parable). I couldn't imagine God would ever call a person a "**virgin**" who had <u>never</u> known God or had never had a **POINT OF CONTACT** with Him. I can't imagine that. But in Jesus' story **1/2** of the "**virgins**" waiting for the bridegroom

<u>**missed Him**</u> **! ! !**

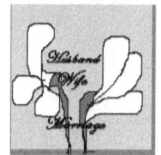

**Oil had run out in their lamps.
The five foolish virgins said to the five virgins that had oil,
"Give us some of your oil." The virgins with oil answered,
"We cannot, or we will not have enough. Go buy your own."
So the five foolish virgins went to buy oil, but while they were
gone, the bridegroom came. When they returned, the door
to the wedding was shut. They could not enter.
It was too late for them forever.**

I know it takes time to let God teach us. It takes time for us to seek Him, find Him, and reach Him. Isaiah 55: 6-7 reads, "Seek the LORD while he may be found, call upon him while he is near: Let the wicked forsake his way and the unrighteous man his thoughts: and let him return to the LORD, and he will have mercy on him: and to our God, for he will abundantly pardon." That is why we gaze upon God, to find a POINT OF CONTACT with Jesus, so the Holy Spirit can have time to seep truth down and into us, watering us like plants, forming in us a special bonding with our Lord.

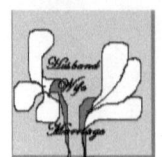

It is vital that we choose to focus on a **true** reflection of God, and have a **real** **POINT OF CONTACT** not an idea of our own making, or we will never be able to form any relationship with the Almighty God. If it's not a true reflection of God that we are gazing at, He won't be there, and if He's not there, we won't form any relationship with Him. God is a person, and He must be there in order

to find a **POINT OF CONTACT** with Him, in order to *"touch"* Him. And He reveals Himself in the part of His creation that we focus on, as we see Him in it. It is a very real way to get to know God in reality! And He reveals Himself in His Word, the Holy Scriptures. And He is Himself, His Word. The Holy Scriptures are the best way to discover God's inner feelings, and let ourselves be taught by Him. God speaks of many issues in His Word, revealing His likes and dislikes, loves and hatreds. So through God's Word, and God's creation, we can find a **POINT OF CONTACT** with God. We can allow Jesus to enter every part of our hearts, permeate us and be a blessing to others through us. I would like to share some

Scripture's that magnify God's Word:

"The law of the LORD is perfect, converting the soul: the testimony of the LORD is sure, making wise the simple. The statutes the LORD are right, rejoicing the heart: the commandment of the LORD is pure, enlightening the eyes. The fear of the LORD is clean, enduring forever: the judgments of the LORD are true and righteous altogether. More to be desired are they than gold, yes, than much fine gold: sweeter also than honey and the honeycomb. Psalms 19:7-11

"For as the rain

comes down,

and the snow from heaven

and does not go back up,

but waters the earth,

and makes it bring forth and bud,

that it may give seed to the sower,

and bread to the eater:

So shall my word be

that goes forth out of my mouth:

it shall not return to me void, but it

shall accomplish that which I please,

and it shall prosper <u>in the</u>

<u>thing</u> to where I sent it."

Isaiah 55:10, 11

*Blessed is the man
that walks not in
the counsel of the ungodly,
nor stands in the way of sinners,
nor sits in the seat of the scornful.
But his delight is in the law of the
LORD; and in his law
he does meditate day and night.
And he shall be like a tree
planted by the rivers of water,
that brings forth his fruit
in his season;
his leaf also shall not wither; and
whatever he does shall prosper . . . "
Psalms 1:1-3*

Personal Notes, Thoughts

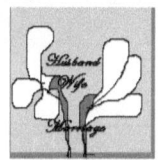

When a **POINT OF CONTACT** has been made with God there is a releasing of ourselves to Him and He to us. Truth flows to us and through us, into us and out of us. There are no aggravations or tensions. There is a sweet peace. There is a freshness, like a breath of fresh air. There is a sense of newness and a sense of simplicity, like being a child again. There is a sense of wonder, because we see and know our Heavenly Father and our great God in the tiniest things, and in things that are huge and gigantic. A **POINT OF CONTACT** happens in an **atmosphere** of *Trust in God*, like our earth is always being held in an envelope of air, the atmosphere.

atmosphere: *n* [ML *atmosphaera*, fr. Gk *atmos* vapor + *sphaera* sphaera]

1 a: the gaseous envelope of a celestial body (as a planet) **b:** the whole mass of air surrounding the earth **2:** the air of a locality **3:** a surrounding influence or environment **4:** a unit of pressure equal to the pressure of the air at sea level **5 a:** the overall aesthetic effect of a work of art **b:** a dominant aesthetic or emotional effect or appeal

atmospheric *adj* **1 a:** of, relating to, or occurring in the atmosphere **b:** resembling the atmosphere: AIRY **2:** having, marked by, or contributing aesthetic or emotional atmosphere

(VAPOR) + (SPHERE) = ATMOSPHERE

God is in the heavens with His wife the Holy Spirit, as the atmosphere surrounds the earth.

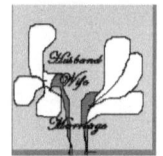

(VAPOR) + (SPHERE) = ATMOSPHERE

SO PERHAPS TRUST IS LIKE THE VAPOR AND
THE KNOWLEDGE OF GOD IS LIKE THE SPHERE.
AIR SURROUNDING THE EARTH IS LIKE THE HOLY
SPIRIT WHO IS COMPARED TO WIND, BY JESUS.
THE EARTH IS GOD'S GOOD CREATION, WHICH SPEAKS
OUT THE KNOWLEDGE OF GOD CONTINUALLY. THIS IS
ALLEGORICAL TO THE MARRIAGE OF THE KNOWLEDGE
OF GOD TO TRUST IN GOD, AS IF THE HEAVENS,
THE ATMOSPHERE, WERE MARRIED TO THE EARTH.
THIS CAN REMIND US OF OUR
DEAR HEAVENLY FATHER AND THE HOLY SPIRIT,
♥♥♥ HIS PRECIOUS WIFE IN THE HEAVEN-LEES ♥♥♥

"Haven't you known?
Haven't you heard?
Hasn't it been told you
from the beginning?
Haven't you understood from the
foundations of the earth?
<u>It is</u> he that sits upon the circle of the earth, and the inhabitants of it <u>are</u> as grasshoppers; that stretches out the heavens as a curtain, and spreads them out as a tent to live in: That brings the princes to nothing; he makes the judges of the earth as vanity."
Isaiah 40:21-23

"Yes,
they shall not be planted;
yes,
they shall
not be sown:
yes,
their stock shall not take root
in the earth:

and he shall also blow on them,
and they shall wither,
and the whirlwind
shall take them away
as stubble."
Isaiah 40: 24

"To whom
then will you compare me,
or to whom
shall I be equal?
says the Holy One.
Lift up your eyes on high, and
see who
has created these <u>things</u>,
that brings out their host by number:
he calls them all by names
by the greatness of his might,
for that <u>he is</u> strong in power;
not one fails."
Isaiah 40:25-26

Yes, God is married. How could He not be? He created man in His <u>own mirrored</u> image,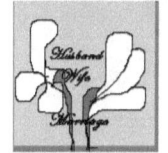

❧ Husband and Wife ❧

"And God said, Let us make man in our image, after our likeness:..."

> "*So God created man*
> *in his own image,*
> *in the image of God*
> *created he him;*
> *male and female*
> *created he them.*
> *And God blessed them . . .*"
> *Genesis 1:26,27*

So God is male and female, a married couple in the heavens. If this were not so, then God would be a liar. God cannot lie, so He truly made man husband and wife, in His own

MIRRORED IMAGE

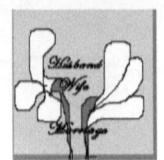

God's intimacy in the heavens with His wife the Holy Spirit, is the most precious and pure expression of love. That's why blaspheme of the Holy Spirit, God's wife, is the only unpardonable sin. God is honoring, protecting, and defending <u>His own wife</u>. God in the heavens in marriage, is love's greatest expression because intimacy in marriage is the most pure, innocent, dynamic, dramatic, and passionate expression of love. And He <u>did</u> make "man in His own image," a <u>perfect mirrored image</u>, male and female, husband and wife. In the next Scripture we see God "**confirmed <u>it</u> by an oath:**" and it is "**impossible for God to lie**", Hebrews 6:17-19: "In which God, willing more abundantly to show to the heirs of promise the immutability of his counsel, confirmed <u>it</u> by an oath: That by two immutable things, in which <u>it was</u> impossible for God to lie, we may have a strong consolation, who have fled for refuge to lay hold on the hope set before us: Which hope we have as an anchor of the soul, both sure and steadfast, and

which enters into that within the veil; where the forerunner is for us entered even Jesus."

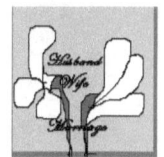

We can seek a **POINT OF CONTACT** with God through this new **Knowledge of God** and also gain a new **Trust in God** and dependency on Him. "The Marriage of the **Knowledge of God** to **Trust in God**" is an analogy of God's marriage in the heavens. In these relationships, each are dependent on the other. Also the atmosphere and the earth are an analogy of both and are similarly dependent on each other. In all the relationships, neither exists without the other. If the heavens existed alone it would have nothing to surround and protect. If the earth existed alone it would have no protection. If **Knowledge of God** remains alone it is a foreigner to God and forms no **POINT OF CONTACT** with Him, no relationship in us with the Almighty, and forms no releasing of ourselves to Him, or intercommunication with Him. If **Trust in God** remains alone it has no protection against false ideas, leading to dangerous spiritual relationship <u>not</u> founded in God, but in Satan:

> **"<u>I Know</u> the blasphemy of the which say they are Jews, and are not, but are the synagogue of Satan."**
> **Revelation 2:9**

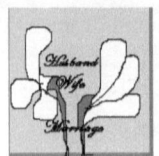

When God becomes our *all in all*, then we may...

knowing

He accepts us

and **knowing we are well-pleasing to God,** not because of what we do, or haven't done, but because we have received Him into our hearts and minds, in the true

Knowledge of God. We have *escaped* ourselves, by filling up with God,

> **being satisfied,**
> > **more than satisfied,**
> > > **much more than satisfied,**
> > > > **saturated with satisfaction,**
> > > > > **overflowing with the satisfaction,**

of knowing Him alone.

Now we just rest in Him.   ♥   Simple as that.

- AND HE FLOWS THROUGH US
- IN VARIOUS INPIRATIONS AND ACTIVITIES

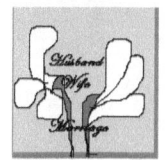

So we let our whole beings come to a quiet place,

Knowing we don't have to do anything to be accepted by

♥ **Him** ♥

<u>*Knowing He is well pleased with us*</u>

because we live in Knowledge of God and Trust in God

because we are honoring Him,

because we are:

letting Him be our ... *Life,*

because we are

letting Him be our... *Delight,*

And He will truly delight us forever!!!

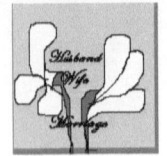

LORD, let us *escape*.

Please let us *escape* ourselves to worship you, and you alone.

God, You are love.

When you fill us up with <u>yourself</u>,

You fill us up with <u>your</u> tender love. ♥♥♥

As we read, "Now the end of the commandment is...

LOVE OUT OF A PURE HEART,

and <u>of</u> a good conscience, and <u>of</u> sincere and genuine faith: (Timothy 1:5).

We have just begun,

just begun to know the depths of your love.

♥ We have begun to "touch" You, ♥

begun to know real love, <u>which is</u> *YOU*

You are everything, Oh God !

Our imaginations cannot fathom,

all the glories into which You will bring us!!!

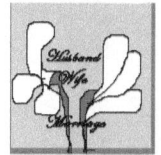

<u>*Forever and ever and ever...*</u>

So let the marriage of us
    to our God,
        begin and never end.

A constant flow of Him to us,
        and us to Him,

A continual filling
    of the Knowledge of God,
    into every atom of our beings,

And our beings fully releasing
        ourselves to Him in a perfect,
        undisturbed Trust,

        forever and ever and ever…..

Epilogue: Husband and wife wash each other with God's Word.

Epilogue: Husband and wife wash each other with God's Word.

Epilogue

> Epilogue: Husband and wife wash each other with God's Word.

In studying the Holy Scriptures to gain Knowledge of God and Trust in God we can earnestly remember that *we are washed by the living Word of God,* and in so doing can gain a **POINT OF CONTACT** with God. This is just like housecleaning, or taking a bath. As we live in our houses and clean them and live in our bodies and cleanse them, so also the Holy Spirit cleanses our minds, hearts and emotions through the Holy Scripture. In the relationship between husband and wife, who we know were created in the very image of God, Scripture teaches them to be washed through the Word of God by letting...

ᙡ *Jesus sanctify and cleanse them with the Word of God* ᙡ

"...Awake you that sleep, and arise from the dead, and Christ shall give you light. See then that you walk circumspectly, not as fools, but as wise, redeeming the time, because the days are evil. So be not unwise, but understanding what the will of the Lord is. And do not be drunk with wine, in which is excess; but be filled with the Spirit; speaking to yourselves in psalms and hymns and spiritual songs, singing and making melody in your heart to the Lord; Giving thanks always for all things to God and the Father in the name of our Lord Jesus Christ; submitting yourselves one to another in the fear of God. Wives, submit yourselves to your own husbands, as to the Lord. For the husband is the head of the wife, even as Christ is the head of the church: and he is the savior of the body. Therefore as the church is subject to Christ, so let the wives be to their own husbands in everything. Husbands, love your wives, even as Christ also loved the church, and gave himself for it *that he might sanctify and cleanse it with the washing of water by the word* that he might present it to himself a glorious church, not having spot, or wrinkle, or any such thing; but that it should be holy and without blemish. So ought men to love their wives as their own bodies. He that loves his wife loves himself. For no man ever yet hated his own flesh; but nourishes and cherishes it, even as the Lord the church: For we are members of his body, of his flesh, and of his bones. For this cause shall a man leave his father and mother, and shall be joined to his wife, and they two shall be one flesh. *This is a great mystery: but I speak concerning Christ and the church.* Nevertheless let every one of you in particular so love his wife even as himself; and the wife see that she reverence her husband." (Ephesians 5:14-33).

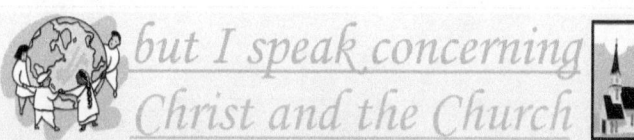 

but I speak concerning Christ and the Church

"Who has directed the Spirit of the LORD, or *being* his counselor has taught him? With whom took he counsel, and *who* instructed him, and taught him in the path of judgment, and taught him knowledge, and showed to him the way of understanding? See, the nations *are* as a drop of a bucket... All nations before him *are* as nothing; and they are counted to him less than nothing, and vanity."

Isaiah 40: 13-15, 17

"And the guitars, and the violins,

the drums, and wind instruments,

and wine, are in their feasts:

but they do not regard the work of the LORD,

neither consider the force

and power of his hands.

Therefore my people are held captive by others,

because <u>they have</u> no knowledge:

and their honorable men <u>are</u> starving to death,

and their multitude shriveled with thirst.

Therefore hell has enlarged herself,

and opened her mouth without measure:

and their glory,

and their multitude,

and their magnificence and splendor,

and he that rejoices,

shall descend into it."

Isaiah 5:12-14

"And in that day
you shall say,
LORD, I will praise you:
though you were angry with me,
your anger is turned away,
and you comfort me. I see,
God _is_ my salvation;
I will trust, and not be afraid:
for the LORD JEHOVA
is my strength
and _my_ song;
he also is become my salvation.
Therefore with joy you shall draw
water out of the wells of salvation.

"And in that day
you shall say,
Praise the LORD,
call on his name,
declare his doings among the people,
make mention that
his name is exalted.
Sing to the LORD;
for he has done excellent things:
this is known in all the earth.
Cry out and shout,
you inhabitant of Zion:
for great <u>is the</u> Holy One of Israel
in the midst of you." Isaiah 12

Oh Zion,

that brings good news,

get up into the high mountain;

Oh Jerusalem,

that brings good news,

lift up your voice with strength;

lift it up be not afraid;

say to the cities of Judah,

Look at your God!

See, the Lord GOD will come with

strong <u>hand</u>, and his arm shall rule for

him: see, his reward <u>is</u> with him,

and his work before him."

Isaiah 40:9,10

"He shall feed his flock

like

a shepherd:

he shall gather the lambs

with

his arm,

and carry <u>them</u>

in his bosom,

<u>and</u> gently

lead those

that are with young."

Isaiah 40:11

Come to me,

all you that labor

and are heavy laden,

and I will give you rest.

Take my yoke upon you,

and learn of me;

for I am meek and lowly in heart:

and you shall find rest to your souls.

For my yoke is easy,

and my burden is light."

Matthew 11:28-30

*"For do I now persuade men,
or God?
Or do I seek to please men?
For if I yet pleased men,
I should not be the servant of Christ.
But I certify you, brethren,
that the gospel
which was preached of me
is not after man.
For I neither received it of man,
neither was I taught it,
but by the revelation of
Jesus Christ."*

Galatians 1:10-12

Now I say, That the heir, as long as he is a child, is no different than a servant, though he is lord of all: But he is under tutors and governors until the time appointed of the father. Even so we, when we were children, were in bondage under the elements of the world: But when the fullness of the time was come, God sent forth his Son . . . God has sent forth the Spirit of his Son into your hearts, crying Abba (Daddy), Father. So you are no more a servant, but a son." Galatians 4:1-7

"For you are not come to the mount that may be touched, and that burned with fire, nor to blackness, and darkness, and tempest, and the sound of a trumpet, and the voice of words: which <u>voice</u> they that heard pleaded that the word should not be spoken to them anymore: ...But you have come to mount Zion, and to the city of the living God, the heavenly Jerusalem, and to an innumerable company of angels, To the general assembly and church of the firstborn, which are written in heaven,

*and to God the Judge of all,
and to the spirits of just men
made perfect,
and to Jesus the mediator
of
the new covenant,
and to the blood of sprinkling,
that speaks better things
than that of Abel.
See that you do not refuse him that speaks.
For if they did not escape who refused
him that spoke on earth, much more
we shall not escape, if we turn away
from him that speaks from heaven."
Hebrews 12:18-19, 22-29*

And what shall I more say?
For the time would fail me to tell
...of David also, and Samuel, and of
the prophets: Who through faith
subdued kingdoms, wrought
righteousness, obtained promises,
stopped the mouths of lions, quenched
the violence of fire, escaped the edge of
the sword, out of weakness were made
strong, waxed valiant in fight, turned
to flight the armies of the aliens.
Women received their dead raised to life
again: and others were tortured, not
accepting deliverance; that

they might obtain a better resurrection: And others had trials of <u>cruel</u> mocking and scourging, yes, even more, of bonds and imprisonment: They were stoned, they were sawn in half, were tempted, were slain with the sword: they wandered about in sheepskins and goatskins; being destitute, afflicted, tormented: Of whom the world was not worthy: (☺) they wandered in deserts and <u>in</u> mountains, and <u>in</u> dens and caves of the earth. And all these, having obtained a good report through faith . . . "Hebrews 11: 32-3

Personal Notes, Thoughts

Thoughts about The Knowledge of God

Thoughts about The Knowledge of God

- ***Knowledge of God*** is wholesome and always right!
- ***Knowledge of God*** is pure and clean!
- ***Knowledge of God*** is bright and inviting and beckons me forever!
- ***Knowledge of God*** is without sin!
- ***Knowledge of God*** is inspiring and invigorating!
- ***Knowledge of God*** is healthy!
- ***Knowledge of God*** is eternal!
- ***Knowledge of God*** is always giving!
- ***Knowledge of God*** is always healing!
- ***Knowledge of God*** is always full of life!
- ***Knowledge of God*** is always king!
- ***Knowledge of God*** is always forgiving!
- ***Knowledge of God*** is always brand new!
- ***Knowledge of God*** is always heartening!
- ***Knowledge of God*** has no death!
- ***Knowledge of God*** is always exciting!
- ***Knowledge of God*** is always good!
- ***Knowledge of God*** is always acceptable to God!
- ***Knowledge of God*** is astounding!
- ***Knowledge of God*** is tender!
- ***Knowledge of God*** is sweet!
- He is always inviting!
- He is always accepting me!

- He is always kind!
- He is always forgiving!
- He is always loving me!
- **Knowledge of God** goes on forever!
- There is never any end to God!
- There is no death in God!
- There is no sadness in God!
- There are no disappointments in God!
- There is only beauty in God!
- There is no lust in God!
- There is no unfaithfulness in God!
- There is no breaking of covenants in God!
- God doesn't change marital partners!
- His wife is the Holy Spirit forever!
- God's love is amazing!
- God loves me tenderly!
- **Knowledge of God** is free for everyone!
- **Knowledge of God** is always available!
- God is always ready to have a relationship with us, if we enter through trust!
- **Knowledge of God** sets me free!
- **Knowledge of God** is fantastic!
- **Knowledge of God** is comforting!
- God always sees me as pure!

- God always loves me!
- **Knowledge of God** is comforting!
- **Knowledge of God** is redeeming!
- **Knowledge of God** is life giving!
- **Knowledge of God** is the answer to all of life!
- **Knowledge of God** has no darkness!
- **Knowledge of God** has no condemnation!
- **Knowledge of God** is powerful!
- **Knowledge of God** is astounding!
- **Knowledge of God** excites me forever!
- **Knowledge of God** lets me rest in his arms!
- **Knowledge of God** gives me new life continually!
- **Knowledge of God** takes away all fear!
- **Knowledge of God** is the source of all life!
- **Knowledge of God** sets me free from all human ailments!
- **Knowledge of God** releases me from all my failures and misjudgments!
- **Knowledge of God** sets me free from all who would seek to control me!
- **Knowledge of God** is tender!
- **Knowledge of God** lifts me up!
- **Knowledge of God** sets me free from all Satanic wickedness!
- **Knowledge of God** sets me free from the evil of my flesh nature!
- **Knowledge of God** sets me free from all the evil of mankind!
- **Knowledge of God** is always new to me!

- ***Knowledge of God*** is always fresh and clean!
- ***Knowledge of God*** is always tender, loving, and forgiving!
- ***Knowledge of God*** is a wonder of wonders!
- ***Knowledge of God*** is incredible!
- ***Knowledge of God*** is my best friend!
- ***Knowledge of God*** is my only friend!
- ***Knowledge of God*** is the meaning to all of life!
- ***Knowledge of God*** is never ending!
- ***Knowledge of God*** is my everything!
- ***Knowledge of God*** sets me up high!
- ***Knowledge of God*** is the center of my being!
- ***Knowledge of God*** is always with me!
- ***Knowledge of God*** has nothing to with human endeavors!
- ***Knowledge of God*** releases me from all traps!
- ***Knowledge of God*** is my hero!
- ***Knowledge of God*** releases me from any difficult situation even if I caused it!
- ***Knowledge of God*** lifts me high above the skies!
- ***Knowledge of God*** makes life and everything about life worthwhile!
- ***Knowledge of God*** is easy to get for anyone, regardless of social standing!
- ***Knowledge of God*** has always been there for me!
- ***Knowledge of God*** is eternally refreshing!
- ***Knowledge of God*** has no boundaries, nothing stops it!
- ***Knowledge of God*** sets me free forever!

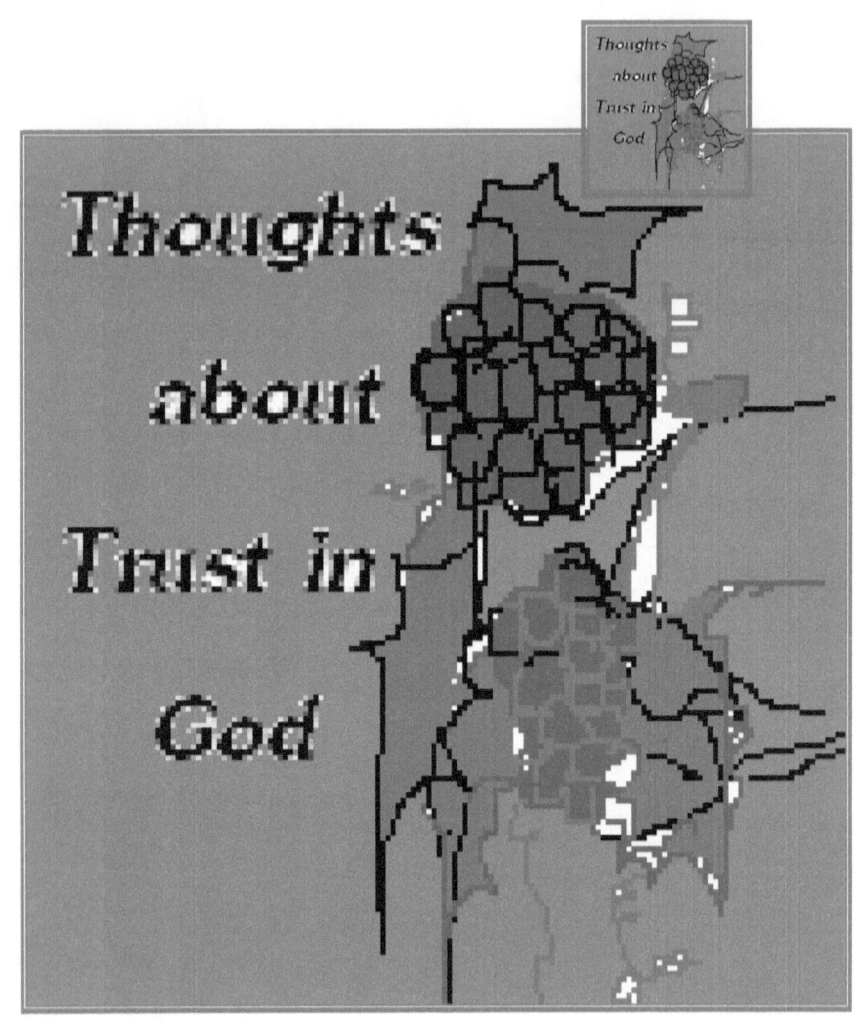

- Trying to get something that someone else has, is not **Trust in God**
- The scripture says, "They entered not in because of unbelief"
- No faith, always is sin. No faith = sin "Whatever is not of faith is sin"
- Where there is sin, there is no **Trust in God**
- Where there is **Trust in God**, there is no sin
- If sin appears or is ignited, it is because there was no **Trust in God**
- If someone enters into sin, it is because of unbelief, no **Trust in God**
- If someone begins to desire what is not theirs, that is not **Trust in God**
- God wants us to know that He is husband and wife in the Heavenlees
- "So God created man in his own image, in the image of God...
- created he him; male and female created he them." (Genesis 1)
- Adam said, "This is now bone of my bones, and flesh of my flesh...
- she shall be called Woman, because she was taken out of Man"...
- Therefore shall a man leave his father and his mother, and shall cleave to his wife:....
- and they shall be one flesh. And they were both naked, the man and his wife,...
- and were not ashamed." (Genesis 2)
- **<u>God created man, husband and wife as a perfect MIRRORED reflection of Himself</u>**
- Father God is the husband and the Holy Spirit is His wife
- "In the beginning God...and the Spirit of God moved..."
- Jesus said, "He that blasphemes the Holy Spirit never has forgiveness."
- Jesus said, "All other sins will be forgiven of mankind."
- This is God's protection of His wife, the Holy Spirit
- A wandering mind, is a lack of **Trust in God**

Thoughts about Trust in God

- Fear, is a lack of **Trust in God**
- Dread, is a lack of **Trust in God**
- Living under the curse of the law, is a lack of **Trust in God**
- Being enticed to wrong thinking by others, is a lack of **Trust in God**
- Praising others, is for the purpose of what God has done in them
- **Trust in God** doesn't ask for a new way, but returns to God, true life
- In the heart of Isaiah, chapters 36-39, the evil king always attacks **Trust in God**
- Sin is like a machine that measures **Trust in God**: when it goes up, trust is down
- Any dread or fear of losing what God has given me, is not **Trust in God**
- Fear is evidence of lack of Trust in God - it shows I am not in **Trust in God**
- God is the one that gives all truth, reveals all truth, including unseen truth
- God says in Isaiah, "In returning and in rest you shall be saved."
- Mary sat at Jesus feet listening to him, and learning from him.
- Her sister Martha was irritated and complained, "Make her help me."
- Jesus answered, "One thing is needful and Mary has chosen that good part..."
- He continued, "which shall not be taken away from her."
- How could this be true, that only <u>**one**</u> thing is needful?
- Because Jesus was meaning, **TRUST IN GOD** and **KNOWLEDGE OF GOD**
- A church can think that they are doing well, but if they do not have **Trust in God**...
- then they have and are nothing, for without **Trust in God** there is no life
- If something is wrong, declare it quickly and openly; expose evil
- Once evil is exposed, God can bring the cure. Trust in God is the cure
- **Trust in God** is the cure for everything

- **Trust in God** is the cure for all evil, for God cannot be tempted
- **Trust in God** brings rejoicing in God
- **Trust in God** is God's life flowing through us, not our lives flowing through us
- **Trust in God** is simply the release of self to God, and total dependence on Him
- **Trust in God** is simple, it is not difficult or hard to do, a child naturally trusts
- **Trust in God** lifts us up into the Heaven-lees
- **Trust in God** is not meditating on our own thoughts but instead, on God Himself
- **Trust in God** never has to turn around in its heart, and go the other way
- **Trust in God** is always going in the right direction, towards God
- **Trust in God** is an ever-unfolding adventure with God
- **Trust in God** doesn't say, "How can I get more from God?"
- **Trust in God** says, "How can I get to know God more and trust Him more?"
- There is no emptiness in **Trust in God** because it is full of God
- **Trust in God** will break all chains of Satan and self-indulgence
- Anything that helps us to release **Trust in God** is good
- We do not learn to **Trust in God** by breaking His commandments
- We do not learn to **Trust in God** by doing unrighteousness
- We do not learn to **Trust in God** by putting our will above His
- We learn to **Trust in God** by saying, "If God wills, we will do this or that."
- **Trust in God** says, "I want to know what is in God's heart, mind, and desires."
- **Trust in God** says "I want to experience God's heart, mind, and desires in me."
- **Trust in God** doesn't stare upon sorrow, but **Trust in God** stares upon God
- **Trust in God** is full of God's beauty - we become a funnel, a conduit for God's glory

- There is no disheartening in God, and so no disheartening in **Trust in God**
- **Trust in God** is simple and available to everyone without exception
- **Trust in God** isn't, "Me, me, me." But, "**GOD, GOD, GOD**."
- God loves **Trust in God** because it makes the kingdom of God available to everyone
- There are no prerequisites to **Trust in God**
- There is no waiting to be better, or more effective, before **Trust in God**
- **Trust in God** in God is immediate, a releasing of oneself to Him, Jesus
- When a wicked man turns to God, every evil he has ever done is "forgotten"
- In the "instant" that a nation turns to God, He removes His pronounced judgments
- **Trust in God** is the answer to every question
- As Jesus said when he appeared to a man on his death bed,
- "You don't have any problems, all you need is faith (trust) in God."
- It is not **Trust in God** when, "...they do not regard the work of the LORD neither...
- consider the operation of his hands. Therefore are my people...
- gone into captivity, because they have no knowledge." (Isaiah 5:12,13)
- I see God is my salvation, I will trust and not be afraid
- for the LORD JEHOVA is my strength and my song..." (Isaiah 12:2)
- "Surely shall one say, in the LORD I have righteousness and strength
- and all that are incensed against him shall be ashamed." (Isaiah 25:24)
- Trust in the Lord forever, for in the LORD JEHOVA is everlasting strength." (Isaiah 26:4)
- Jesus said, "Have faith in God,"
- "I will also leave in the midst of you an afflicted and poor people...
- and they shall trust in the name of the LORD." (Zephaniah 3:12)

Thoughts about Prayer to aid waiting on God

Thoughts about Prayer to aid waiting on God

- Waiting on God is my favorite thing to do
- He makes me all shiny new
- I like to wait quietly in His precious presence
- He never condemns me
- He always lifts me up and encourages me
- He always delivers me
- He always delivers me from any powers stronger than I am, that want to hurt me
- He always restores me
- He always moves deep within me and fixes me
- I like to go to Him because He always accepts me freely
- God never turns me away
- God is my friend.
- He is dear to me.
- I like to come into His presence
- I like to know He loves me
- I like to feel as if I'm with Him throughout eternity even if only for a few minutes
- I like to talk to God if I have something real to say to Him
- I like to talk to God if I have something to truly say from my heart
- I like to know God
- I am pleased that I can come to the Almighty without getting burned up
- That makes me happy to be free and safe in His presence
- I enjoy the privilege of coming to Him
- I enjoy the honor of coming to Him

Thoughts about Prayer to and waiting on God

- I greatly rejoice in God my king
- Waiting at his altar is precious
- God is mighty
- We will wait on Him forever
- We will never grow tired of Him
- We will never grow bored of Him
- From God springs all life
- So waiting at His altar brings a future of mysterious beauty
- Mysterious because all conceivable life comes from Him
- Mysterious because God does anything he wants to and no one can tell Him not to
- Mysterious because He may go against all the conventions of man
- Mysterious because He makes "foolish the wisdom of the world..." (1 Corinthians 1:20)
- He "turns wise men backwards and makes their knowledge foolish;" (Isaiah 44:25)
- He "calls those things that are not as though they were." (Romans 4:17)
- Mysterious because "the haughtiness of man shall be bowed down..." (Isaiah 2:11)
- Mysterious because He accepts me
- I like being with my quiet, loving, Father
- I like and love learning about Him
- I like to cuddle up to My Heavenly Father
- I like to curl up inside of Him
- God likes to listen for my voice
- God moves by his Spirit when I speak words of faith from an honest heart
- I like to pray with others at church prayer meetings

Thoughts about Prayer to and waiting on God

- I love to see God move to help others as we pray for them
- I love for God to use me to pray for others
- I love the excitement of seeing lives renewed and smiles back on sad faces
- I believe God moves by His power through believing prayer
- God listens, God answers the humble, He waits to hear our cry
- God is our source of rest and peace and we may seek for Him through prayer
- Waiting on God brings me nearer to God
- Waiting on God makes me feel humble and childlike
- Waiting on God helps me sense and believe in my need for Him
- Waiting on God helps me know about my full and utter dependence on Him
- Waiting on God makes me quiet, makes my soul quiet, and quiets confusion
- Waiting on God is an escape route for otherwise unbearable situations
- Waiting on God releases one from one's tensions and the tensions of others
- Waiting on God can make one humble so God would feel free to move in him.
- Waiting on God releases from the expectations of others to seek God's expectations
- Waiting on God releases a quietness into the soul that nothing else can do
- Waiting on God brings one into the innocence of a child, like revisiting childhood
- God says, "wait on the LORD, the Holy One of Israel, in truth." (Isaiah 10:20)
- God has been waiting, "the remnant shall return... to the mighty God." (Isaiah 10:21)
- Waiting on God is sweet and comforting, like a baby in its mother's arms
- Waiting on God is daily exercise, "on you do I wait all the day." (Psalms 25:5)
- "It is good that a man should both hope and quietly wait for the salvation of the LORD." (Lam.3:26)
- "I did not say to the seed of Jacob, Seek me in vain." (Isaiah 45:19)

- Waiting on God is an earnest way to unveil one's desire to seek Him
- Waiting on God may not be approved by others, but is welcomed by God
- Waiting on God rescues of us in times of danger, hurt, and sorrow
- Waiting on God brings a hunger "Set your affection on things above..." (Colossians 3:2)
- Waiting on God brings God down to earth, "as in heaven, so on earth" (Luke 11:2)
- "The Lord direct your hearts...into the patient waiting for Christ." (2 Thessalonians 3:5)
- Waiting on God is the answer to our inability to rise above our frailties
- Waiting on God releases us from the demanding and overpowering flesh nature
- Simple honest prayer brings the power and deliverance of God into us
- Trusting Words to God allows Him to do mighty things in us
- Words to God from a heart of Trust in God is true communication to a true God
- Words to God from a heart of Trust in God, in Jesus' name brings God on the scene
- Words to God from a heart of Trust in God brings creative miracles from God
- Words to God from a heart of Trust in God changes the world
- Words to God from a heart of Trust in God is building up, restorative, and healing
- Words to God from a heart of Trust in God takes us out of our self-made boundaries
- Words to God from a heart of Trust in God releases us into God's presence and beauty
- Words to God from a heart of Trust in God relaxes us to do true work in God's kingdom
- Words to God from a heart of Trust in God puts man off the scene, and God on the scene
- Words to God from a heart of Trust in God heals and binds up deep, bleeding wounds
- Words to God from a heart of Trust in God takes us into eternity on wings of victory...
- through clouds of doubt, confusion, disappointments, and desperate failures...
- into his great and glorious love, brightness and peace forevermore with Him

Personal Notes, Thoughts

(THOUGHTS) + (POETRY) = THOUGHTOETRY

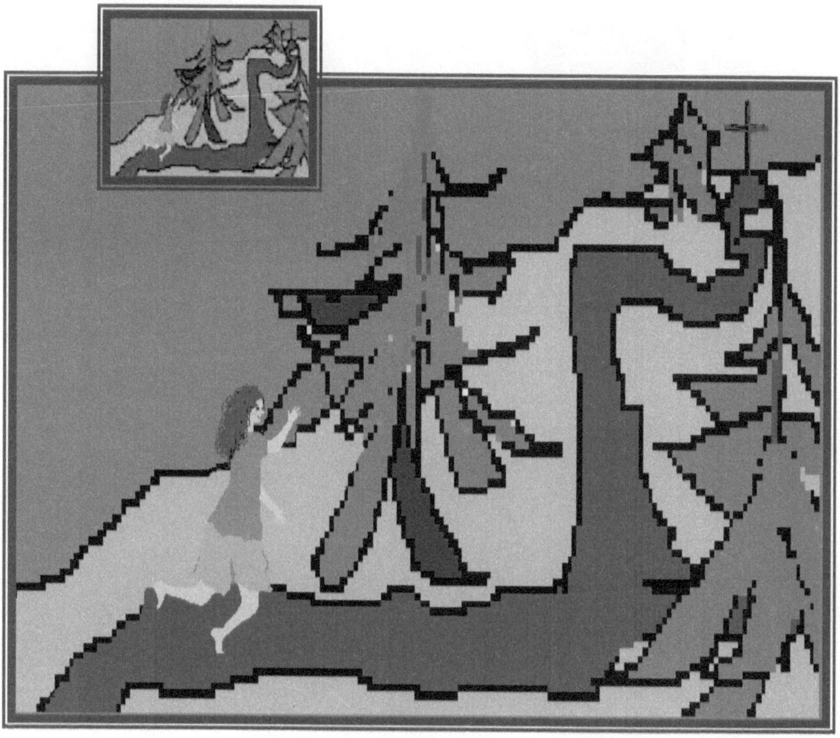

Dear Heavenly Father,
I ask that you would give me
something to say to you from a
heart of trust.
I wait on you forever.
In Jesus' name I ask,
Amen.

(THOUGHTS) + (POETRY) = THOUGHTOETRY

Dear Heavenly Father,
I ask that you would give me
something to say to you from a
heart of trust.
I wait on you forever.
In Jesus' name I ask,
Amen.

Thank you, oh God, for what words can do, spoken in trust by your Spirit in us.

We know you created everything by the words of your mouth.

Please let us be sensitive to your Holy Spirit, that we will only speak the words that your Holy Spirit gives us to say, and that we may be in your image as you created us to be, using the power of our tongues only as you would have us, for your glory, to let you establish your kingdom in this world through our mouths, through the words of trust that your Spirit speaks through us, as you graciously give us the words to say.

Thank you Father,
In Jesus' name,
Amen.

*I would like to call this
section*

(THOUGHTS) + (POETRY) = THOUGHTOETRY

*because it is
thoughts mixed with a flavor
of poetry*

<u>You</u> know dear
LORD,

<u>Exactly</u> what
words...

Words can give harmony to families so their family life can be full, ordered and exciting like a symphony, with many unexpected turns, surprises, much energy, and times of soothing quietness, gaining power and suspense and ending with incredible victories and accomplishments.

<u>*You*</u> *know dear*
LORD,
<u>*Exactly*</u> *what*
words...

...will bring
    families,
        into maximum

    unity.

Words can bring tenderness, warmth, gentleness and God's compassion, and bring God's tender mercy and loving heart into our lives, minds, and emotions.

<u>You</u> know dear
LORD,
<u>Exactly</u> what
words...

...will carry
your love,
to a dying

world.

Words can give wisdom to the Shepherd to guide and care for His flock, to lead them to rivers of living water, to feed them with honey from the rock, the body and blood of Christ, the Words of God, full of the Spirit that quicken the dead and seek for the lost, bring back those that were driven away, bind up the broken, and strengthen the weak.

<u>You</u> know dear LORD, <u>Exactly</u> what words...

...will care

for your

flock.

Words – GOD GIVEN – are the expression of His person and when full of the power of His name, will carry His person to all parts of the earth so we will rejoice in His person and no other person.

<u>You</u> know dear

LORD,

<u>Exactly</u> what

words...

...will bring
your person into us,
and cast out
ALL idols,

eternally.

Words can create trust in Jesus, in the human heart; a divinely inspired dependence on our allpowerful, mighty God; they can release us from self-dependence, all anxiety, and unexplainable attacks on our mind, causing us to enter into a quiet rest, as a newborn on it's mother's breast.

You know dear
LORD,
Exactly what
words...

...will encourage us to rest in you,
    undisturbed forever,
        in the center of your heart,
            with never the slightest care,
                in perfect oneness with you,
                    forever and ever and

        ever...

Words can bring God's prosperity filtering, and flowing into every avenue of our lives, in body, mind, soul, spirit, finances, earthly goods, necessities, and God given pleasures, causing us to abound in every good thing, that we may reach out to others without reluctance, and share the ever-unfolding magnificent bounties of our loving Heavenly Father.

<u>*You*</u> *know dear*
LORD,
<u>*Exactly*</u> *what*
words...

...will give Your exceeding success,
    to come plunging into our lives,
        that we might always
           be pouring out
                Your blessings to

        others.

Words can carry the
        presence of God.

<u>You</u> know dear
LORD,
<u>Exactly</u> what
words...

...will enlighten my darkness,
and bring the fullness,
      of the Holy Spirit,
        into my

      being.

Words can cleanse,
    and root out evil.

<u>You</u> know dear
LORD,
<u>Exactly</u> what
words...

...will loosen me,
    from the bondages of Satan,
    and the flesh nature,
      into your love and

    peace.

Words are power.

<u>You</u> know dear
LORD,
<u>Exactly</u> what
words...

...will bring about
 the changes
  that You want
   in my

  life.

Words are connectors.

> *You know dear*
> *LORD,*
> *Exactly what*
> *words...*

...will

    connect

        us

           more

        intimately.

Words carry the power of God.

<u>You</u> know dear
LORD,
<u>Exactly</u> what
words...

...will accomplish
Your works,
in the earth,
that You

desire.

Words can bring refreshing of the Holy Spirit, water in the desert, and the springing up of fountains from the deep.

<u>*You*</u> *know dear*
LORD,
<u>*Exactly*</u> *what*
words...

...will

    give

        drink

           to

              your

           people.

Words can draw families, communities, nations, and the world together.

<u>You</u> know dear
<u>LORD</u>,
<u>Exactly</u> what
words...

...will bring unity,
    and wholeness,
        into our relationship

        networks.

Words can bring God's beauty, preservation, balance, and harmony.

<u>You</u> know dear
LORD,
<u>Exactly</u> what
words...

...will loosen
    God's glory
        and perfection,
      into the

      earth.

Words can bring safety, security, protection, soundness, and seclusion from all evil.

<u>*You*</u> *know dear*
LORD,
<u>*Exactly*</u> *what*
words...

...will protect your flock,
    and keep them from harm,
        and out of harm's way,
           in your tender
              and strong

        hand.

Words can build your church, lift up your people to heights untold, and cause us to do exploits and wonders for you.

<u>You</u> know dear
LO<u>R</u>D,
<u>Exactly</u> what
words...

...will
    open
        heaven
            up.

Words can bring knowledge, understanding, insight, and new ideas and ways to solve problems.

You know dear
LORD,
Exactly what
words...

...will bring the
fullness of,
your precious

revelations.

Words can cause us to treasure and cherish one another, and honor and respect each other, while encouraging and appreciating one another.

<u>You</u> know dear
LORD,
<u>Exactly</u> what
words...

...will express
and place,
your <u>priceless worth</u>,
on each

individual.

Words can bring life to the world, bring God's Kingdom down from above, and the carrying out of God's will in the earth.

<u>You</u> know dear
LORD,
<u>Exactly</u> what
words...

...will bring the
manifestation
of the Sons of

God.

Words can bring the men and women of God into the full development of their characters and bring them into levels of glory with God that no one has ever dreamt possible; can unveil God's secret hidden treasures, and "rip open the belly of heaven" causing His wonders to cascade into the earth like a giant heavenly waterfall.

<u>You</u> know dear
LORD,
<u>Exactly</u> what
words...

...will
    burst open,
        the heart of

            heaven.

Words can bring the lifting of heavy burdens, the lightening of everyday dreariness, and the loosing of those caught in destructive habits.

<u>You</u> know dear

LORD,

<u>Exactly</u> what

words...

...will

    set

        your

           people

        free.

Words can bring your light into a dark place; they can expose and release God's little ones from habitations of cruelty.

<u>You</u> know dear
LORD,
<u>Exactly</u> what
words...

...will
    bring
        Your beautiful
            children.
                out of the
                    Devil's

    playgrounds.

Words can bring people up from the dead, pull them out of the pit, and rescue them from damnation.

<u>You</u> know dear
LORD,
<u>Exactly</u> what
words...

...will bring God's
    favor,
        and love,
            and carry,
                the healing

body and blood of Christ.

Words can bring the treasuring of old memories, and the shining of the pearls of God's previous works in the earth.

<u>You</u> know dear
LORD,
<u>Exactly</u> what
words...

...will solidify
    our acceptance,
        of your reality,
           and warm,
                our hearts with

    remembrances.

Words can bring healing.

> <u>You</u> know dear
> LORD,
> <u>Exactly</u> what
> words...

...will bring your healing balm,
    soothe the broken-hearted,
        comfort the wounded,
           and heal hearts
              and minds,
                emotions and

relationships.

Words can bring fruitfulness, development of talents, fruition of giftings and maturity of a godly character.

<u>You</u> know dear LORD, <u>Exactly</u> what words...

...will
    bring
        us
            into
                the
                    100-fold

harvest!

Words can bring stability, order, cleanliness, and a new way of living.

<u>You</u> know dear
LORD,
<u>Exactly</u> what
words...

...will bring the
    perfect manifestation
        of the Word of God,
           into your life,

        in me.

Words can bring tenderness, warmth, gentleness and God's compassion, and bring God's tender mercy and loving heart into our lives, minds, and emotions.

<u>*You*</u> *know dear*
LORD,
<u>*Exactly*</u> *what*
words...

...will give
    your workers,
        HARVEST
            TOOLS!!!

Words can get people back on track, back into God's blueprint, back on God's drawing board, back into their DESTINY, back into God's promises, back into His covenant with man, back into the personal covenants that God has made with them.

<u>*You*</u> *know dear LORD,* <u>*Exactly*</u> *what words...*

...will get each person back, into their God given

destiny.

Words can bring childlike simplicity and truth back into our lives.

> *<u>You</u> know dear*
> *LORD,*
> *<u>Exactly</u> what*
> *words...*

...will release and flood,
    our inner courses with joy,
      allow us to be free,
        with the wonder of a child,
       and find joy
         in the simplest,
          and smallest things,
           of God's good

      creation.

Words can expose the heart of God, the depth of His inner compassion for mankind, His continuous seeking for the lost, and His bleeding passion to draw men to Himself.

<u>*You*</u> *know dear*
LORD,
<u>*Exactly*</u> *what*
words...

...will expose
your inner,
crying

for us.

Words can cause twisted minds to unwind and conform to God's plan, wounded souls bruised with abuse from the evil one to be completely restored, and those traumatized from defective, destructive, and distorted thinking to be reinstated into healthy mental patterns of thought.

You know dear
LORD,
Exactly what
words...

...will reform
and renew,
the inner
recesses of

man.

Words can cause the Devil to have to give up the goods he has taken, the blessings he has stolen away, the properties he has illegally confiscated out of the hands and possession of God's people.

> *<u>You</u> know dear*
> *LO<u>R</u>D,*
> *<u>Exactly</u> what*
> *words...*

    ...will cause
        the Devil
            to give it up,
                and spit it

            out!

Words can bring complete wholeness to a marriage and keep partners in infinite wonder of the expression of God manifested through them; they can bring romance that never dulls, passion that always burns, understanding that is tender, a closeness that is ever present, a joy that is effervescent and bubbling and life giving.

You know dear

LORD,

Exactly what

words...

...will give a bubbling spring of life,
to a marriage,
that always runs

full.

Personal Notes, Thoughts

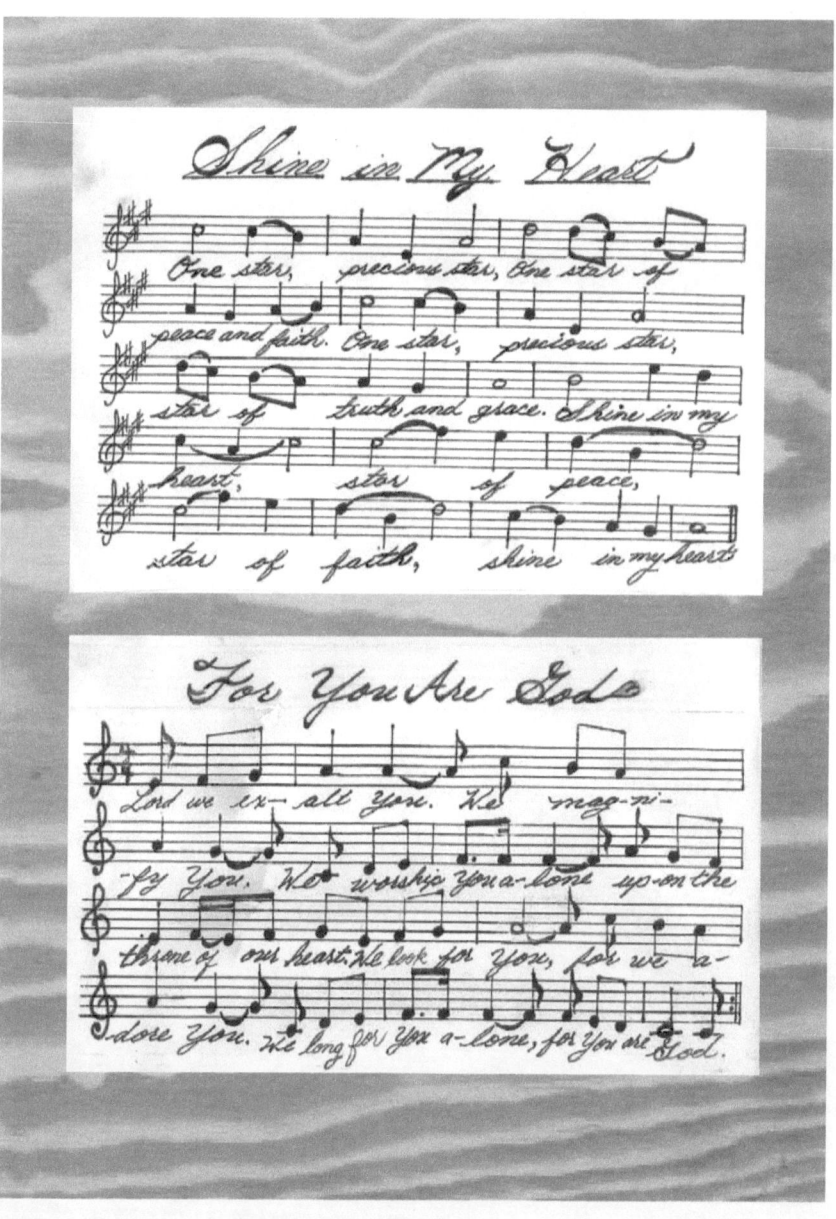

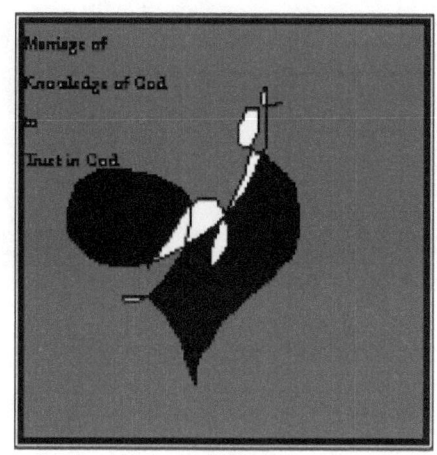

L.L.L.

Jesus said,
"I am Alpha and Omega,
the beginning and the ending,
says the Lord,
which is, and which was,
and which is to come,
the Almighty."
Revelation 1:8

www.ingramcontent.com/pod-product-compliance
Lightning Source LLC
Chambersburg PA
CBHW030543080526
44585CB00012B/243